HEAVEN
IN YOU

& YOU
IN HEAVEN

Unveiling Eternity on Earth

HEAVEN IN YOU

& YOU IN HEAVEN

Unveiling Eternity on Earth

ELIZABETH M. KELLY

the WORD
among us®
press

The Word Among Us Press
9639 Doctor Perry Road, Ijamsville, Maryland 21754
www.wordamongus.org
12 11 10 09 08   1 2 3 4 5
ISBN: 978-1-59325-119-2

Cover design by DesignWorks Group

Library of Congress Cataloging-in-Publication Data
Kelly, Liz, 1967-
  Heaven in you and you in heaven : unveiling eternity on earth / Elizabeth
M. Kelly.
     p. cm.
  ISBN 978-1-59325-119-2 (alk. paper)
  1. Heaven--Christianity. 2. Catholic Church--Doctrines. I. Title.
  BT846.3.K45 2008
  236'.24--dc22
                          2008009759

Contents

For Joseph, whose heart is so open, it has no doors.

We are travelers, traveling to our homeland, and we despair of reaching it, in our despair we faint. But he whose will it is that we should reach the homeland where he will keep us, nourishes us upon our journey.

—St. Augustine of Hippo

Acknowledgments

The author wishes to acknowledge:

Patty Mitchell, whose thoughtful comments and guiding eye has greatly improved this work.

My mother and father: Being with you so much this past year has been one of the most precious gifts of my life. Thank you for taking delight in me, for encouraging me in my gifts, and for letting me borrow so much of your hope on those occasions when my reserves were overdrawn.

To all the wonderful women of my world: Cristia, Pamela, Heather, Lil, Anna, Mary, Mother Mary Emmanuel and the Sisters of the Visitation in Tyringham, along with the Rome contingent, Jona, Mary, Suzi, and my dear Molly (Miss Fitzgerald), on whose kitchen table at Via Insannio this work was completed. Your friendship, prayers, wise counsel, and support keep me walking upright.

My professors in Catholic studies at the University of St. Thomas and the Angelicum in Rome: My faith is stronger and deeper, richer and more real for all you have taught me. I am so grateful for your lives, the great ardor you have for your respective fields, your generosity in sharing all you know, and your commitment to the teaching life.

Bill, my third brother: Thank you for your prayers.

Lauren and Nicole: Thank you for your fashion and photo consultation and for all those nighttime prayers you offer for your aunt. You make life so much more enjoyable. I am proud of you and the young women that you are becoming. Don't ever forget how much God loves you and delights in you.

Jon: If there is any hope that I am learning to give myself increasingly with "an undivided heart," it is due much to your example. Thank you for living with constancy and with spiritual courage.

And Joe: Sometimes there is no way to describe or even comprehend the way one's heart must go to unveil that deep gaze of the Beloved, but I treasure the knowledge that our hearts so frequently seem to visit that same soul-place, "although by night." I love and admire you more than you know, and by the grace of God, should I arrive in heaven one day, I'm sure it will be long after you. Please, don't forget me, put in a good word for me, and if you can, save a spot close, close by for your sister.

I.

Opening Exhortation:

Let's Go to Heaven

He has made everything beautiful in its time. He has also set eternity in the hearts of men; yet they cannot fathom what God has done from beginning to end.

—Ecclesiastes 3:11 (NIV)

Here on earth, we are called to look up to heaven, to turn our minds and hearts to the inexpressible mystery of God. We are called to look toward this divine reality, to which we have been directed from our creation. For there we find life's ultimate meaning.

—Pope Benedict XVI

Come to think of it, it's a rather bold proposal to write a book on heaven. It's only natural to wonder about one's credentials for such an endeavor.

The question was first posed to me directly on a quiet, country road. I was walking with my dear friend, Anna, a Schoenstatt sister and an extraordinary, accomplished woman in her own right. We were catching up after years apart, and she asked me what I was writing about now.

"Heaven," I said.

"And what do you know about heaven?" she asked. My dear Anna, always the practical German, has a wonderful way of getting straight to the point.

Having just begun my research on the topic, I laughed aloud and answered, "Precious little, I'm discovering."

It was a legitimate, useful question, and I thought about it a long while afterward. *What do I know about heaven?* I've never been there. I'm not a mystic, not a theologian or scholar.

On the other hand, do we have to experience something first-hand in order to form accurate thoughts about it? Much of our life knowledge is actually gathered through observation and the experience of others. We look at bugs under microscopes and at the stars through telescopes and have formulated volumes of ideas—truths even—about them without becoming bugs or stars, without personally experiencing "bugness" or "starness." Similarly, a man can formulate a few ideas about pregnancy and motherhood, though he will never become pregnant. Plenty of women have something to say about the meaning of fatherhood though they will never be fathers.

As I continued to research and study, I discovered that this question—what could any of us really know about heaven?—was the great opening caveat to nearly every book I read on the topic. We have obvious limitations. But it also reminded me of G. K. Chesterton's intriguing thought: "Mysticism keeps men sane. . . . The ordinary man has always been sane because the ordinary man has always been a mystic. . . . The whole secret of mysticism is this: that man can understand everything by the help of what he does not understand."[1] And already, the centerpiece for this book was this verse from Ecclesiastes: "He has made everything beautiful in its time. He has also set eternity in the hearts of men; yet they cannot fathom what God has done from beginning to end" (3:11). The work of pondering heaven and all that entails, then, is perhaps not as much tied to facts to be measured and recorded on paper as to sit with open awe in the presence of its mysteries and allow its light—incomprehensible and burning though it may be—to fill in the face of the earth and the hearts of humankind, leaving no crevice, no crack, no corner darkened.

Surely, entomologists could tell you more about bugs and astronomers more about stars than I could about either. And though we cannot put heaven under a microscope and no telescope exists that will reach the face of God, there are those whose lifework is studying heaven; this book trusts their wisdom. The Mass is glorious instruction on the work of heaven; I attend often and with as much awareness as I can muster. The communion of saints and angels certainly has a vested interest in the topic; I beg their intercession, particularly the Blessed Mother. Scripture and Church teaching on the matter is exquisite, and I trust in and meditate upon it as well.

Ultimately, I believe what Jesus teaches about his coming kingdom, even in those instances where it falls far beyond my comprehension. I trust that eternity is in me and I am in eternity, and that I will be made beautiful in God's time. I trust that he meant what he said to the thief, "Today you will be with me in paradise," and that in a way, when we choose heaven, when we are moved to the point where we recognize Truth, each one of us is that thief. And we all have a responsibility to learn the language of heaven, to become fluent in the mother tongue of eternity. Astronomy has not been set in my heart, but eternity has; I must honor this with a life ordered toward the coming of his kingdom. Every Christian life must become an open, ongoing study of eternal life.

Your Kingdom Come on Earth as It Is in Heaven

When Peter said, "Lord, to whom can we go? You have the words of eternal life" (John 6:68), he was teaching us something that is very important as we set about to contemplate heaven. He was teaching us that there are things we *can know* about heaven. There are aspects of eternity that we can discern and adopt and live out to bring about God's kingdom on earth. In the teaching of Jesus, in God's creation, in the love of the Father, and in each one of us, eternity is made manifest. I am discovering in this work—this ordinary woman contemplating extraordinary heaven—that his kingdom comes to earth in beauty and glory and faith. His kingdom comes when we practice mercy and justice. It is expressed in community—angels and saints and humankind. It is lived out in our homes and in our hearts. It is given skin and bones in our holy joys and even in our sufferings and sorrows. And it is celebrated in sabbath rest, when we are poised in stillness, face to face with Jesus, when we know that *he is God* (see Psalm 46:10).

What I am beginning to believe is that maybe I have been to heaven. Maybe you have been, too. Maybe we "go" there more frequently than we realize. Maybe heaven is all around us and we simply do not acknowledge it. What did the novelist Marcel Proust say? "The real voyage of discovery consists not in seeking new landscapes but in having new eyes."

How, then, to acquire heavenly vision, eyes informed by eternity, the perspective of paradise? How to nurture and mature this heart made for eternal dwelling places?

IMAGINING ETERNITY

In the first place, we might need to take our imaginations out of the closet and dust off the cobwebs. We Catholics could do much more to utilize our imaginations and creativity. We've become imaginatively slothful. Compliance and control are *big* in our big, adult world. And sometimes, I think, it makes us fearful of our own imaginations. Imagination is essential when we contemplate heaven, imagination fed by faith and reason. Heaven is one of the greatest places that Catholics can let their imaginations run, not "wild," as in out of control, but run "in the wild," as in "run in our natural habitat." Heaven is our natural home, but we've shrugged off this idea like so much deadwood.

Pope Benedict XVI writes that our current crisis of faith is really "a crisis of Christian hope."[2] That is, we've lost a Christian imagination intimately linked and in love with eternity. As our imaginations shrink and shrivel, so does our belief in a lavish, generous God who occupies a beautiful, glorious, joyful heaven where he accounts for each hair on your head.

In his Letter to Artists, Pope John Paul II writes, "May the beauty which you pass on to generations still to come be such that it will stir them to wonder! Faced with the sacredness of life and of the human person, and before the marvels of the universe, wonder is the only appropriate attitude."[3] What a marvelous exhortation, and doesn't it tell us so much about his personal delight in the human imagination, particularly when it has surrendered itself to the Holy Spirit? To contemplate heaven, we must enlist and trust and enliven our God-given capacity for "wonder."

With freshly invigorated imaginations in tow, we now come to the real work. Pope John Paul II will long be remembered for this perpetual exhortation to his flock; repeating the words of Jesus, how often he said, *Do not be afraid.* He believed that the great legacy of the twentieth century was not progress, not technology, but fear. He also wrote that "the Christian ought to live in the perspective of eternity."[4] How are you doing with those two assignments? Do you see how closely they are related, like two sides of the same coin?

This book is written for those of us who live perhaps more often in fear of the future than in faith in all things, seen and unseen. It is written for those of us who fail occasionally or often to live, day in, day out, with eternal perspective, soul's eyes fixed beyond the veil. This book is written as a means to encourage one another in the truth that all things are made beautiful in their time. This book is written for those who have been worn down with cynicism such that they can no longer imagine heaven, neither in their minds nor in their hearts. It is written in happy anticipation of a new heaven and a new earth, not as an escape hatch from life's difficulties and disappointments, but as fulfillment of the promises of our loving God and the completion and perfection of all creation, including me, including you, and because *heaven is true*.

St. Francis de Sales exhorted us to pray often, "whenever you can, and in whatever setting, always seeing God in your heart and your heart in God."[5] I would add that, whenever we can, and in whatever setting, we need to see heaven in our hearts and our hearts in heaven, as impossible and fearsome as that may seem at times. As I sit here and write, I pray earnestly that God will increase my powers of observation and bless me with an interior, Spirit-filled view of you, right there, where you are: *you in heaven and heaven in you*. Like the blind beggar, I plead, *Lord, Lord, I want to see*.

A tenderhearted woman I know signs notes to her husband with this closing: "Let's go to heaven!" Maybe it seems innocent and affectionate enough on the surface, but really it's quite profound when you think about it. It is a gentle and wise reminder of not only our earthly assignment—to help one another get to heaven—but an honest, joyful, and bold exhortation to unceasingly align and realign our daily perspective with this mystery, this reality, this promise of eternal life. It is the bold proposal we must all undertake. That is exactly what is at stake. May this book serve as the same kind of encouragement, one more tiny pebble of light cast out into the human pond.

My fellow saints in the making, my pilgrim brothers and sisters, do not be afraid. Let us live with eternal perspective. Let's go to heaven.

1. G. K. Chesterton, *Orthodoxy* (New York: Image Books, Doubleday, 2001), 23–24.

2. Pope Benedict XVI, *Spe salvi*, Vatican City: Libreria Editrice Vaticana, (30 November 2007): 17.

3. Pope John Paul II, Letter to Artists, Vatican City: Libreria Editrice Vaticana, (4 April 1999): 16.

4. Pope John Paul II, *Fear Not* (New York: Barnes & Noble Books, 2000), 10.

5. Francis de Sales, Letter 217, to Madame Boulart, May 3, 1604, *Classics of Western Spirituality: Letters of Spiritual Direction* (Mahwah, NJ: Paulist Press, 1988), 103.

2.

Heaven as Home

Heaven does not belong to the geography of space, but to the geography of the heart.

—Pope Benedict XVI

Home interprets heaven. Home is heaven for beginners.

—Charles H. Parkhurst

It was late June when a delivery man from the airlines drove up to the house. I was living on my family's farm in rural Minnesota, and my dear friend Cristia had flown in for a visit. Her bag had been lost in transit, and this gentleman was returning it to her from the Minneapolis airport, at least an hour's drive from all things "city." As he got out of the van and began walking to the front door, I watched as he turned literally in circles, his eyes sweeping across the landscape of our property, which was lush with the green of midsummer. He moved toward me slowly, his mouth slightly open, like he'd been pleasantly stunned. I thought he might be confused as to whether or not he had the right address—we are somewhat off the beaten path—so I inquired, "May I help you?"

He set the bag down a few feet in front of me as though he were exhausted and simply could not go on. He put his hands limply on his hips, took one more intense look around, let out a deep sigh, shook his head slightly, almost in disbelief and said, "It's like a little slice of heaven out here."

It is a common response to our modest hobby farm. Countless visitors have used the exact same phrase to describe it. I smiled to myself and thought, "Sir, that's exactly why I'm here." How fortunate was I to be able to come here to pen a book on paradise.

But what do people mean when they say, "a little slice of heaven"?

Let me fill in the picture of our home just a little more.

The farm is situated on about fifteen acres alongside a little river several miles from the nearest paved road. The half-mile driveway is lined with trees, their branches drooping low over the drive. Just at the end, they break open to reveal our big red barn, complete with a green and yellow John Deere tractor, a grotto dedicated to Our Lady of Grace and St. Michael the Archangel, the garage (which holds the chapel above it), and the farmhouse perched on a knoll, the main log cabin of which was built in 1857. The original beams inside still reveal the craftsmanship of the hands that chiseled and shaped and molded without the aid of electricity. No power tools touched that wood.

The original smokehouse still stands, too, though barely, along with an old hitching post. The yard is large and opens with a full view of fertile, rolling farmland and the tree-lined river that winds along the back line of the property. A windmill—when employed—clips along, gathering up brisk currents of air. The farm hosts a veritable menagerie of animals, too: horses and chickens and ducks and kitties and the world's most affectionate border collie—my nieces named him Sparky. Each animal has its own personality. Our roosters, for example, crow at odd hours of the day and night. We like to say that they must think they are living in a different time zone; they think they are chickens on holiday from Singapore.

The house is surrounded by huge oak and elm trees; an old swing hangs from one branch. My brothers have planted maples and dogwoods, apple trees, rose bushes, and a large garden.

But that's just what you can see. Here's some of what you cannot "see." Prayer is a high priority here. Family Rosary and the Daily Office are common affairs. Before my older brother leaves in the evening for his home in the city, he bows his head before my dad to receive his blessing in the name of the Father, Son, and Holy Spirit. The house has been repainted a beautiful rich blue in honor of the Blessed Mother—we think of it as "her color." My brother and dad used the wood from an old granary to build parts of the chapel, including the altar. To sit in our chapel during Mass on a bench made of wood that is more than a hundred years old as our resonant, if slightly off-key, alleluias drift heavenward is . . . well, heavenly.

But what does that mean? Why do we say that, "a little slice of heaven"? What is it about *this* place that reminds us of *that* place, a place we've never been, a place that, logically speaking, we really should have no memory of at all? This little patch of land in anonymous, rural Minnesota is our home; why does it stir the imagination in the direction of paradise?

The Geography of Home

Let's assume for a moment that our home life has been healthy and good (and certainly for some, this is not the case, but we will address that later). After a long trip, we might cross the threshold and sigh, "It's good to be home." Why is that? What are some of the more common, positive associations with "home"?

For one, being home often means our work is finished and we can now rest. I'm certain our delivery driver was at least in part struck by the peace, quiet, and general pastoral beauty of our farm. He didn't look like he was excited to return to traffic and city noise and the busy day that lay ahead. Home means rest.

We often associate "home" with a sense of security or safety. In this rural area, when local children ride their bikes to the swimming pool, they leave them piled on a grassy knoll outside, no bike rack, no bike chains, no bike locks anywhere in sight. "Home" assumes a certain amount of protection; you can let your guard down.

"Home" frequently means comfort, nourishment, and familiarity. A friend of mine who travels as many as two hundred days out of the year says his favorite part about traveling is coming home to sleep in his own bed and eat healthful meals he's prepared himself in his own kitchen. A roof over our heads serves as protection and as a place where we can gather together with those we most treasure, those we know; it is a sheltering place of inclusion. And true homes seem always able to accommodate more, to take in those who are far from home or have no home at all.

When we are home, our joys, pleasures, sorrows, and wounds are comfortably housed and understood; we are known; we are revealed and revealing without fear of "exposure." Surely, "home" means belonging—it means family and community. "Home" knows us and we know "home." We know the language spoken there; we know its customs and the intimacies of family humor, the "inside jokes." When we feel or make ourselves "at home," we relax and become most ourselves.

When we invite visitors in, we say, "Make yourselves at home." In our house, that means, "Go ahead and rummage through the fridge or pantry if you're hungry, stretch out on the couch if you want to nap, browse the books on the shelf if you want to read, or take a walk in the woods—we have plenty of extra hats, gloves, shoes, jackets, bug spray." When visitors, especially children, come to our farm, my mother opens the door and says, "Hi there, I'm Grandma." Not, "Hi, I'm Grandma Kelly," not, "Hi, I'm Elizabeth's mom." What my mother means when she says, "Make yourself at home," is "You are welcome to become, even if for just a day, a part of our family—brother, sister, mother, father, daughter, son, grandchild. You belong, and what we have is yours."

How much more so will this posture of welcome, of home, be magnified in heaven? When we pray as Jesus taught us, "Our Father, who art in heaven," we are recognizing that our Father, the head of our eternal household, has made his home in heaven, and however ideal our earthly homes may be, they are only a mirror, a shadow, of what is to come. Philosopher Peter Kreeft captures this notion when he writes, "the 'more' is *infinitely* more; thus the analogy is not proportionate. Twenty is to ten what ten is to five, but infinity is not to twenty what twenty is to ten, or five, or one. But it *is* 'in that direction,' so to speak."[1] Maybe our little farm is "in that direction," and this is what visitors find so compelling.

At times we might be tempted to think in terms of heaven somehow mirroring earth, but really, this is backwards: earth is analogous to heaven. The best we experience of earth, heaven is better, *infinitely* better. The most joy we experience of earth, heaven is more joyful, *infinitely* more. The deepest love we feel here, heaven is deeper, *infinitely* deeper. The most we feel "at home" on earth, we will feel perfectly at home, *eternally at home* in heaven. Day by day, this is what our farm is teaching me: that the universal desires for home and for heaven are intimately linked, because in the Christian life, home and heaven are the same. And we are all designed, we are all "in the direction of" being most ourselves, being most at home; we are designed as heaven-dwellers.

I open with discussion of *this* place for the very reason that it does remind so many of *that* place—that city called heaven. I open with this earth, this farm, because it is the reality I know. I open with this place because it is where I have been given to pray, "My Father, who is at home in heaven, your kingdom come, your will be done on *earth*—this earth, right here, right now—as it is in *heaven*." In other words, *Lord, may we come home, may we enter your will. Lord, make your home with us.*

And I open with this place because I believe that God uses every circumstance of our lives, no matter how minor or coincidental they may appear on the surface, to draw us to him, to bring us home to heaven.

You Can Go Home Again

The phrase is familiar: "You can't go home again." I understand what it means philosophically, metaphysically; but when it comes to our eternal home, the notion does not apply. In fact this is, in some ways, the trajectory of the Christian life, to return home to our Creator. The work of the Christian life is to move toward our great restoration, moving back home, continually returning ourselves in thought and spirit to eternity, as Pope John Paul II urged us, to live with the perspective of eternity. We were born out of the superabundant love of an eternal being; dwelling in eternal love is our best fit, the best form for our lives. It bears itself out occasionally in our earthly lives to remind us that heaven is our true home; if we choose it, we can be restored to our eternal heritage. We can be restored from exile.

My childhood was spent in the country, not too many miles from here on a farm very similar to our current one. Our family of nine lived on a few acres of woods near a river lined with cottonwood trees. There was plenty of room for wandering around, exploring, or fishing with my little brother for bullheads, carp, and sunfish, the local fish fare. We had horses, apple trees, and a sprawling garden.

My nature has always tended toward introversion, so it was a natural fit to spend hours outside alone, picking violets and Dutchman's Breeches, or out in the barn, grooming my horses, or riding empty old roads. One of my favorite things was sweeping out the barn at night, a simple and satisfying task. To this day, I still love to sweep, probably because it recalls the simple pleasures of that part of life; it reminds me of every good thing.

At that time, in childhood, living in the country was my greatest joy, greatest safety, the place I felt most myself, the place where I was most "at home."

Then, rather reluctantly, my family moved when I was thirteen. Leaving the farm to live in town was devastating for me because it meant giving up all that was familiar and beloved, my horses and hours in the woods. Life in town was lonely. God was certainly with me and brought me numerous gifts, like music, to replace my beloved farm, but I always felt the loss, the way you feel the loss of things that make childhood feel safe and meaningful and joyful. These losses were a very natural part of life, but they also precipitated a greater awareness that I was entering into a kind of pilgrimage, an exile. I found that I was always just a touch under the weather with homesickness, missing our farm, always feeling a little out of place. But our God is a mighty God, a God of restoration and homecomings.

This summer, the summer I am writing this book, my Father in heaven has brought me home again, and more. Living here on the farm, my days frequently consist of Mass and adoration, praying the office with my brother who is on break from seminary studies, praying the Rosary or Divine Mercy Chaplet with my family, writing, personal prayer, study, and riding horses with my nieces. Sometimes we have evening prayer in our chapel, fashioned by the hands of men that I love, men who love God, men who long for heaven. That child-joy of home has been restored to me—and magnified. After nearly thirty years, God has brought me here: to this little slice of heaven. And it is even better than before. Even more.

And even so, it is still just a slice, a sliver, a crumb. The "more" of heaven—that eternity that our Creator has impressed upon my heart and yours—will be *infinitely, eternally* more.

GRIEVING HEAVEN

My favorite time for horseback riding is late in the evening. After a day's writing, with the winds dying down and evening's calm descending, I head for our big red barn and saddle my brother's horse, a black Arabian Saddlebred named Shadow. We wander along the river accompanied by Sparky, perhaps the most athletic creature God ever created, who flushes out a startled menagerie of pheasant, turkey, rabbit, and deer. Sparky also acts as our pace car from time to time, cantering along beside us when we pick up some speed, challenging Shadow to race. Then we amble up out of the trees and out onto old country roads to meander among fields of corn, beans, and grazing cattle.

The summer sun sets late in Minnesota. In midsummer, we watch it dip below a horizon, dressed in silos and fields and groves of oak trees, casting pink hues across the open Midwest sky, a fading watercolor. With evening breezes, the corn leaves tip over along the top, like glossy, green fingers rolling in a lush wave. An eagle has made its nest in a tree alongside the creek, and we occasionally see him gliding above us, authority and confidence taking flight. And God is magnified.

On evenings like these, the world is gentle and at peace, and the joy I feel at God's creation swells in my heart and mind. His perfect presence and great love is palpable, like wildflowers to be plucked and gathered up in your arms, their sweet scent drawn deeply into your lungs. But then the moment passes, as all things on earth do. It has been said that "time is just another word for death." Paradoxically, in this passing away, this dying, even as it stirs my awareness of God's presence, it also stirs the longing for the completion of that presence, for an *endlessness* of that presence, and I grieve, just a little bit, for heaven. God uses these moments to remind me in his gentle way that I am—we all are—in exile. This infinite desire written across our hearts can only be filled with an infinite being.[2] Until the moment of our "crossing over," we must embrace it: this gentle grief, this gentle longing, like flowers that bloom and fade.

All grief touches that eternal place in us that wants so much to return to the complete company of our Creator, the fullness of our God. It is a part of the plan. When we meditate on heaven, Jeremiah's exhortation to the Israelites is God's exhortation to all of us:

> I will fulfill to you my promise and bring you back to this place. For surely I know the plans I have for you, says the LORD, plans for your welfare and not for harm, to give you a future with hope. Then when you call upon me and come and pray to me, I will hear you. When you search for me, you will find me; if you seek me with all your heart, I will let you find me, says the LORD, and I will restore your fortunes and gather you from all the nations and all the places where I have driven you, says the LORD, and I will bring you back to the place from which I sent you into exile. (Jeremiah 29:10-14)

What promises! What plans! How good a God is this! He will allow the earnest seeker to find him—and then restoration comes, exile ends, and we are brought back. We are brought home.

Holy Alien or Escape Artist?

You *are* in exile, and there will be moments when you will feel it acutely. Intrinsically, in the manner in which God formed us, we own this desire for something or someone, which earthly life does not provide. Peter Kreeft writes, "Who whispered in our ear the desire for heaven? And when? And even more mysterious, why do we understand it? . . . And when and how did we forget it?"[3] These are important questions to ponder because they remind us that God himself has "set eternity in the hearts of men." This impression may be darkened; it may be denied, dismissed, or forgotten. It may even be resented, but it cannot be removed. You have it, I have it—it is universal; we are all intended for eternity.

We may be tempted to chase after a million different loves disproportionately in the mistaken hope that they are heaven-shaped. Sex, money, power, cigarettes, food, television, golf, talking, relationships, work, even riding horses on country roads in the evening or—fill in the blank—none of these sate our desire for God and heaven. A spiritual mentor who helped me greatly with a lifelong struggle with unhealthy eating habits would often say, "We don't look for God in the refrigerator. He doesn't live in there." None of our earthly grapplings, though they may take the edge off our earthly exile, truly make us feel at home. Some will increase our desire for heaven, and those we should continue to practice; some will distract us from our desire for heaven, and we may need to spend time editing them out of our routine. Either way, we will need to become better practiced at sitting with our eternal longing, resting in the knowledge that "alienation" is really a good thing.

Malcolm Muggeridge writes, "The only ultimate disaster that can befall us . . . is to feel ourselves to be at home here on earth. As long as we are aliens, we cannot forget our true homeland."[4] This belief smacks initially of the shrinking of life; it carries a false aroma of reduction and of belittling this pilgrim Church on earth, making it some kind of terrible drudgery to be endured and heaven the eternal escape hatch for all of life's problems and pain. But that's the background noise of contemporary culture yammering away relentlessly. That's materialism and consumerism and plain old vices like greed and lust and sloth sneaking up on you and me. To recognize the homeland of heaven and identify alien earth paradoxically animates our lives on earth and gives them ultimate meaning. We remind ourselves that the Church teaches the reality of heaven not because it is easy to understand, but because it is true. It is what Jesus taught. If we can resolve the initial question—is it true?—then it only becomes a matter of acting accordingly.

Kreeft addresses the reduction to escapism by asking,

Would it be escapism for a fetus to think about birth? Does life after birth make life in the womb any less important? Doesn't it make it infinitely *more* important? . . .

Heaven is not escapist because we are already there, just as the fetus in the womb is already in the world because the womb is in the world and subject to its laws. . . . We are not yet born from the world-womb, but we are already part of the heavenly Body.[5]

A Christian heaven may have fallen out of fashion, even among Christians, but that doesn't change its reality in the least. It is as though we have been walking on the beach of our culture, and try as we may, its sand has worked its way in between our toes. We've lost sight of the vast shores that lay across the waters, spread out before us, a sweeping visual feast of plenty, for the itchy grains in our shoes. Instead, we drop our heads and wiggle our toes in sandy agitation. Maybe we need a good long rinse. Maybe we need to look up and stretch out our eyes more often to eternal horizons. Maybe we need to make heaven more of a daily habit.

"Alien" can be a tough gig, but it's truly the only gig in town for a Christian; and furthermore, when we are honest with ourselves, it's the only gig we really, truly, in our heart of hearts *want*. There's simply no place like home, and until we get there, we must live with a gentle grief, a holy, gentle longing. And, we will discover, deep, deep down, at the very root of our alien grief, that joy is bleeding, seeping out its very lifeblood, generously feeding the root in the places where it is most tender, most vulnerable, most wounded, most thirsty for home.

In her poem "First Love," poet Denise Levertov, a convert to Catholicism, captures this intrinsic longing written across the heart of every human. She draws upon her very first encounter in childhood with a flower, a "pale shell-pink, a chalice / no wider across than a silver sixpence" to say,

It looked at me, I looked
back, delight

filled me as if
I, not the flower,
were a flower and were brimful of rain.
And there was endlessness.
Perhaps through a lifetime what I've desired has always
      been to return
to that endless giving and receiving, the wholeness
of that attention,
that once-in-a-lifetime
secret communion.[6]

We all want to come home. We all know that deep prayer of Moses, "O, Lord God . . . let me cross over to see the good land beyond the Jordan" (Deuteronomy 3:24-25). We all carry the same burden, that holy, God-given longing to return to *endlessness, wholeness of attention,* that place where in *secret communion* with the Creator, we become a little pink chalice, full to the brim. It's heaven.

1. Peter Kreeft, *Heaven: The Heart's Deepest Longing* (San Francisco: Ignatius Press, 1989), 205.

2. Kreeft, quoting Blaise Pascal, 204.

3. Kreeft, 55.

4. Malcolm Muggeridge, *Jesus Rediscovered* (New York: Doubleday, 1979), 47–48.

5. Kreeft, 174.

6. Denise Levertov, *Selected Poems*, ed. Paul A. Lacey (New York: New Directions Books, 2002), 195–196.

3.

HE THEN IS BEAUTIFUL IN HEAVEN

*Beauty is one of the rare things that do not
lead to doubt of God.*

—JEAN ANOUILH, PLAYWRIGHT

*He then is beautiful in heaven, beautiful on earth; beautiful
in the womb; beautiful in His parents' hands; beautiful in
His miracles; beautiful under the scourge; beautiful when
inviting to life; beautiful also when not regarding death;
beautiful in "laying down His life"; beautiful in "taking it
again"; beautiful on the Cross; beautiful in the Sepulchre;
beautiful in heaven.*

—ST. AUGUSTINE OF HIPPO

*How lovely is your dwelling place,
O LORD of hosts!*

—PSALM 84:1

I picked my apartment in a huge hurry. I was only in town for
a few days before I had to head back to Boston to finish up my
work, and I didn't have time to look around. In fact, I only
looked at one place and with only one requirement looming in
my mind: location. After years of commuting on the East Coast,
I knew I didn't have it in me to drive anymore. I had to be within

walking distance of campus. This apartment was two blocks from the Center for Catholic Studies, where I'd be spending much of my time for the next two years. Short of finding a dead mouse on the premises (or some other fur-bearing creature), I had pretty much decided that I would rent the place before I even walked in the front door.

By the time I actually moved back to St. Paul, I had forgotten what the place even looked like, and I was a little nervous as I turned the key in the lock for the first time on my return. But it was fine—not the Ritz, not a cardboard box under the overpass, but happily, somewhere well in between. It had good light, refinished wood floors; it was cozy, tiny, room enough for one, a happy little cloister for prayer and study and writing. And it was two blocks from my future universe, guaranteeing me a virtually car-free life for the next two years. Talk about heaven.

But then—and this is so like the God I am coming to know— there was more.

It was 6:00 p.m. on one of the first evenings I was settling into the apartment. I was exhausted from the move, nervous about returning to school, anxious about not having sold my house in Boston yet, unsure I'd done the right thing in moving back. So many question marks were hanging over my head—in work, in finances, in relationships, in my spiritual life. Amid a small, turbulent sea of half-empty boxes and crumpled, strewn-about wrapping paper, I sat down for a minute and looked out the window into the backyard, praying, "Dear Lord, have I made a mistake?"

There were three towering cottonwood trees, my favorites, looming there, large and ancient, like the Father, Son, and Holy

Ghost to witness my wondering, their massive, knotty arms sprawling heavenward. The sun was gently setting through their thick foliage, a breeze stirring their leaves, that same breeze dancing in through my windows to blow my hair back from my dirty, tired face. Just then, the clock struck six. That's when I first heard them in the background: church bells from the campus chapel, gently tapping out an *Ave*, the melody so beautiful, so familiar and steady, so much "at home" to me, I started to sing along, to pray along, "Triumph all ye cherubim, sing with us ye seraphim. Heaven and earth resound the hymn! Ave, Ave, Ave Maria."

The burdens of the day were lifted, even if they were not removed. My prayers were heard even if they were not clearly answered, and my heart was drawn toward eternity, for heaven announced its presence through that beauty.

A true encounter with beauty—be it the beauty of a gentle melody or the beauty of a gentle breeze—has revelatory power. A true encounter with beauty, by its nature, will draw us to heaven, whence it came; it draws us home, our thoughts and spirits heavenward. Beauty takes us by the hand and delivers us to that meeting place where heaven and earth do resound the hymn. It captures that intermingling where heaven and earth are full of his glory, where visible and invisible worlds breathe the same eternal air, and where truth and goodness take on flesh and bone, the melody and color of this world, and walk around in it, humming heaven's tune. When we have eyes to see and ears to hear, true beauty reveals the Revealer.

A Beautiful Theology

Love is the greatest evidence that heaven is real, but the beauties of earth are a pretty close second, whether they are expressed in nature, in the arts, or in one another. Theologically speaking, most of us are probably fairly comfortable with the idea that heaven sees us, but we struggle with the reverse idea, that we see heaven. Beauty is one of the primary means by which God makes himself present to us. When we encounter real beauty, we're encountering heaven.

Beauty is such a powerful catalyst for living with an eternal perspective that an entire branch of theological study—theological aesthetics—has been developing with this notion in mind. Writing about the work of Hans Urs von Balthasar, one of our foremost thinkers in theological aesthetics, Fr. John Cihak noted, "Balthasar seized upon love revealed in beauty as the path to bring the non-believer to faith. Western culture, having grown tired of seeking truth and goodness, and largely despairing of finding them, could be brought back to the One who is both Truth and Goodness through Beauty." As beauty's great apologist, Cihak said, Balthasar was convinced that "the post-modern heart is still captivated by beauty revealing love, and this may be the road to Christ for many citizens of the post-modern world."[1]

Balthasar is in good company; so many poets and writers and artists have long intuited the notion made famous in Dostoyevsky's novel, *The Idiot*, that beauty will save the world. But what, exactly, is beauty? Aquinas noted that the beautiful should never be an "innocuous sedative," but an evocation of the "good made visible."[2] The beauty of heaven is always accompanied by what Balthasar calls "her two sisters," truth and goodness. They cannot be separated if they are to speak the language of eternity fluently. He writes:

> In a world without beauty—even if people cannot dispense with the word and constantly have it on the tip of their tongues in order to abuse it—in a world which is perhaps not wholly without beauty, but which can no longer see it or reckon with it: in such a world the good also loses its attractiveness. . . . In a world that no longer has enough confidence in itself to affirm the beautiful, the proofs of the truth have lost their cogency.[3]

Balthasar would further argue that beauty is not only the result of truth and goodness and a vehicle to their recovery, but evidence of the superabundance of God's love. Beauty is evidence of a world ordered by a lavish, excessive Lover, pouring out his affections superabundantly, much like the apostles' net, breaking at the overabundance of fish. Beauty is heaven's overflow of love, as though God's love is so great, it simply cannot be contained in heaven; it must flow out over the earth. And beauty is one of the containers designed to hold the excess.

I've lived in some truly beautiful parts of the world, including Alaska. Imagine flying into Anchorage in the middle of winter as the sun sets in early afternoon, casting its faded pink hues across mountains buried in wind-whipped snow; or waking to find the first dusting of snow—"termination dust"—on the mountains in fall; or the rainforest of southeast Alaska with its ancient trees so thick around, you could get lost traveling their circumference; the surprising squish of tundra beneath your feet; Denali on summer solstice, looming and indifferent in the distance until well past midnight, so large, it must intimidate all other creation but maybe the sun. If Alaska isn't evidence that God is obsessed with the beautiful, I don't know what is.

But I will never forget one particular chilly February night when a friend called me very late. I picked up the phone and without announcing herself at all, she simply declared, "I'll be in front of your house in five minutes. Dress warm." I obeyed. Minutes later, we were driving down Seward Highway, headed for a remote perch halfway up the side of a mountain. The northern lights were out.

When we found a good spot away from city lights, we parked and climbed out onto the roof of her truck. There we lay, covered in blankets, long and stretched out, creatures parallel to a living sky, watching as the air high above us caught fire. These were not the recognizable northern lights I knew from postcards. They were not faded, pulsing lights off on the distance of a dark horizon. For over an hour, these lights shot across the whole sky suspended above us, each their own band of spiraling Milky Way, only in color: blue, green, yellow, red. It was nothing short of dazzling.

In that kind of encounter with beauty, that breathtaking kind of beauty, you have to wonder at a God who would bother. What kind of love but a superabundant one would design a world where night skies pulse with color, and those of us with eyes wide and awake and turned toward heaven can share in the celestial dance?

Beauty speaks to a God of transcendence and to creatures designed for wonder. It enlivens our relationship with heaven because it echoes these things. Pope John Paul II writes, "Beauty is a key to the mystery and a call to transcendence. It is an invitation to savor life and to dream of the future. That is why the beauty of created things can never fully satisfy."[4] Instead, he suggests that it "stirs that hidden nostalgia for God which a lover of beauty like St. Augustine could express in incomparable terms: 'Late have I loved you, beauty so old and so new: late have I loved you!'" Dietrich von Hildebrand says it this way:

> As we behold . . . beauty, our heart is filled with a desire for loftier regions about which this beauty speaks, and it looks upward with longing . . . it announces God in its quality . . . it contains a summons; in it there swells a *sursum corda*; it awakens awe in us; it elevates us above that which is base; it fills our hearts with a longing for the eternal beauty of God.[5]

That dazzling night sky drew up more than our eyes; our very hearts were reaching, longing for heaven, answering its constant invitation to love.

That is, to love God, not to love beauty. True beauty, heaven's beauty, points to something beyond itself. It does not stand before a mirror, returning its own vain gaze. It does not stir up a desire to possess, like Eve in the garden, grabbing greedily at the pleasing apple and its vain promises. Real beauty is selfless, serving only as a vessel to point us to a love that does not fail and does not fade: the love of the Father. In our world, so darkened by the utter failure of finite human love, beauty descends to pierce the darkness, to resonate in the deepest, most hidden hallows of the soul and, whether we recognize it or not, to draw us back to Jesus.

Balthasar writes that Christians who are sent into the world to evangelize "are put on the path with authority and with the powers to convince, but these powers do not refer to the ones sent; they refer only to the Lord who is proclaimed." This is also true, he says, in relation to faith, hope, and love; they are "meant to draw people's attention to God's form in the world."[6]

So, too, beauty. It bears the same burden; it has been given the power to convince and the authority to refer to the One proclaimed. Beauty's vocation is to draw people's attention to God's form in the world.

BEAUTY AND THE BEHOLDER

What does an encounter with beauty render in the human heart? "Before the beautiful," writes Balthasar, "no, not really *before* but *within* the beautiful—the whole person quivers. He not only 'finds' the beautiful moving; rather, he experiences himself as being moved and possessed by it."[7] What might this be like?

Imagine (that dangerous word again) that you are in Rome, standing in St. Peter's Basilica before Michelangelo's *Pietà*. At first you are more aware of the swarms of tourists and pilgrims (they are loud and you think perhaps a tad irreverent, buzzing by with barely a glance). But you continue to look, to behold, and gradually these distractions begin to fade away. You begin to take in the lines of Christ's body, the drape of Mary's robe, the curve of her figure that enfolds the Man, the luminescence of heavy marble, set firmly on immoveable earth. You sense permanence, completion. "It is finished" hangs in the air.

You may find yourself particularly drawn to reflect on the face of Jesus. It is turned, you notice, gently toward heaven, still searching for Abba Father perhaps. You try to name his expression written in stone and death. Is it acceptance or peace? You stand on the guard railing in front of you, trying to get closer. Could it possibly be that this beautiful face of death is almost smiling? Is his an expression of joy? You feel suddenly overcome, as though you might like to crawl into the lap of the Madonna and help, somehow, to cradle the Lamb. It is an elegant, mournful sting. A prayer rises up within: "Surely this was the Son of God."

There is a parallel experience between the reception of revelation and the reception of beauty. Beauty, like revelation, captures the intermingling of natural and divine worlds and calls upon the beholder to open and renounce oneself. "The result of the encounter with beauty is the impression of the form on the person."[8] Beauty does not point to itself; it points to God, giving itself up to him completely. In love, through love, true beauty lifts us from the face of the earth that we might catch a glimpse of the face of God.

In his poetry, Rilke suggests that true beauty asks us to change.[9] Balthasar might add that true beauty invites us to pray. The great paradox of the encounter with beauty is that we approach her hoping to receive something from her, and we do. But in relationship with her, we come to understand that beauty asks something of us, too.

BEAUTY CRUCIFIED

The church I attend in St. Paul is appointed with wonderful, rich wood. Most notably, centered high above the front of the nave, just before the altar, hovering on a long, darkly stained beam, are three life-sized wooden carvings: Christ on the cross and, poised on either side, Mary and the apostle John. It is a striking trio, beautiful and dark and sorrowful. You sense, even at a glance, that they hold up the truth, and that truth holds up the world. But you just might miss them if you do not know to look.

One day, on one of my first visits to daily Mass there, I sat very near the front of the church with a friend. It is my habit to make a slight lifting gesture with my hands toward heaven when the priest begins the eucharistic prayers and says, "Lift up your hearts," and the congregation replies, "We lift them up to the Lord." It is my friend's habit to raise not only his hands but also his head. Maybe it was because I was with him that day, but when it came to the prayer, I lifted my hands *and* my gaze, and—I was taken aback. Just at that moment, as we raised our eyes, there was Jesus looking directly back down on us from his cross, looking directly at *me*, standing there in the third pew on the right, anonymous and little and humble and low, attending Mass on a Thursday afternoon. It was palpable, piercing, this being seen, being witnessed and witnessing, and recognizing that indeed, when we lift our hearts to the Lord, that this is precisely where he takes them: *to the cross*. When we raise our eyes and lift our hearts, we not only witness the cross, we agree to participate in it.

That day, Jesus was hanging right there before us, catching our eyes to witness the act, to facilitate the revelation. Eye to eye, there was a promise made, a commitment to be kept. That darkly beautiful work of wooden art helped to magnify the truth of the prayer: *Lift up your hearts; we lift them up to the Lord.* How many thousands of times have I rattled off those words, barely registering their meaning, thinking of a thousand other things. It required an encounter with beauty to magnify, to enliven the truth of heaven such that I could understand and choose to draw closer to Jesus. That day, because I was looking, because I was open to it, beauty lived out its vocation to announce God's form in the world.

The priest begins, "The Lord be with you," and he *is*, even as he is in heaven, too. It is the work of beauty to increase our awareness of this reality. It is the work of beauty to point beyond itself, to point to heaven. It is the work of beauty to bridge heaven and earth, all things seen and unseen. In this, it patterns itself after Jesus, the Incarnate One, and this is what gives it its potential to be so efficacious in the Christian life, the life lived with eternal perspective.

> Beauty is not an extra, it is essential to all existence. . . . It is the splendour of beauty that makes the true and the good whole. The magnitude of beauty in nature and in all human creation, wherever it is experienced, gives us a glimpse of

the beauty of God, and therein lies its saving power . . . and this includes the mystery and glory of Christ on the cross, the utter distortion of divine-human beauty and yet its complete fulfillment. This paradox is the basis of Christian faith and cannot be overlooked.[10]

Beauty, just like its master, asks something of us; it invites us to surrender, even unto death, because that is the way to heaven. "All the way to Heaven is Heaven," said St. Catherine of Siena, "because Christ is the way."[11]

BEAUTY IN YOU AND YOU IN BEAUTY

There's been a great deal written about Blessed Mother Teresa in recent years, some of it attempting to disparage her and her faith in some slight way for living a silent, decades-long "dark night of the soul." From her vantage point in heaven, I've often wondered what she, this tireless mite of a woman who hated the spotlight, this great lover of the poorest, most neglected, most anonymous and forgotten of God's children, must think of all the hubbub. *Dear Blessed Mother Teresa, pray for us.*

With her face splashed prominently across our world's most influential magazines, I've had many opportunities to contemplate it: the deep lines, her bright eyes, a heavy sorrow veiled behind a lifetime of reassuring smiles. How appropriate, too, that when she died, it was her heart, that huge, glorious heart, that had worn out, no doubt from perpetual overuse. Living in protracted dark night or not, she is an absolute beauty. Her life was a work of art, one of heaven's great masterpieces. Nothing is more beautiful, more heavenly, than a life lived in heroic virtue, and surely, she did this.

But our haggard world suffers greatly from "beauty-confusion." We no longer recognize it when we see it. In light of the body-insecurity industry—it has become a multibillion dollar business—it's easy to do. We think beauty lives in looks; we hover over superthin, airbrushed models. We often forget that this is not our definition of beauty, because truth is not there. And this confusion over real beauty has crept into other aesthetic venues, music and art and design. We settle for so much less than what I imagine heaven must have had in mind.

But mostly, I think, we miss the beauty of heaven in one another.

I recently had the opportunity to visit one of the outposts for Blessed Mother Teresa's Missionaries of Charity in Rome. One of the sisters there who spent a good deal of time with Mother Teresa shared a story which demonstrates the dramatic power of a beautiful life. This sister had been working in one of the poorest, most dangerous areas of Rome. She and the other sisters managed somehow to become acquainted with every outcast on the street in that area, but there was one man who resisted their kindnesses. He suffered from addiction and AIDS, and every time they passed him, he would shout obscenities at them, terrifically vile things. Unlike the others, this man's heart never grew any tenderness for the sisters, but following the example of their founder, they continued to reach out to him whenever they could.

Several years before Blessed Mother Teresa's death, she was hospitalized with illness and this news reached all the papers. One day while she was still ill, the sisters passed this man on the street. He ran up to them, assuring them, "Today, I won't say anything bad!" He told them that he'd learned of Mother Teresa's illness, and he was deeply concerned. "I was born in hell, I live in hell, and I'm going to hell," he told them flatly, "but I prayed to God that he would let us keep Mother Teresa longer." Naturally, the sisters were deeply moved by his words and this sudden "conversion," but then he added, "I'm afraid that if she dies, all love will leave the earth."

He died four months later at a home for men run by the Missionaries of Charity. Mother Teresa lived another four years.

He'd never met Mother Teresa, but it didn't matter. A life of beauty has the power to cut through any kind of obstacle: space, time, woundedness, hardness of heart, even hell on earth. Mother Teresa looked at the poorest of the poor and saw absolute beauty because she saw Jesus in them. In turn, the poorest of the poor were given a glimpse of heaven in Mother Teresa and her army of sisters and volunteers. When they looked into the eyes of Mother Teresa, or any one of the Missionaries of Charity, it was heaven that was looking back, an eternity of love meeting them, face to face. And all the beauty that had been lost in them—to drugs, or AIDS, or poverty, or rejection—was found again, and renewed.

What's beautiful in you is God's imprint, and this cannot be removed—not by drugs or illness or tragedy or even sin. It can only be darkened—or illuminated. Cardinal John Henry Newman once wrote,

To those who live by faith, everything they see speaks of that future world; the very glories of nature, the sun, moon, and stars, and the richness and the beauty of the earth, are as types and figures witnessing and teaching the invisible things of God. All that we see is destined one day to burst forth into a heavenly bloom, and to be transfigured into immortal glory.[12]

That means you, too. You are destined to bloom for heaven. You have been created for the true beauty of immortal glory, to witness and teach the invisible things of God, to be the beauty of God's form in the world, and to impress it upon others. And when you do, heaven itself is broken open. It resounds across the face of the earth, familiar and inviting, as clear and bright and beautiful as a chapel bell.

1. John R. Cihak, "Love Alone is Believable: Hans Urs von Balthasar's Apologetics," *Ignatius Insight*, May, 2005, http://www.ignatiusinsight.com/features2005/jcihak_hubapol_may05.asp.

2. Gesa Elsbeth Thiessen, commenting on Kant and Aquinas, *Theological Aesthetics: A Reader* (Grand Rapids, MI: William B. Eerdmans Publishing Company, 2005), 205.

3. Hans Urs von Balthasar, *The Glory of the Lord, Volume 1, Seeing the Form*, trans. Erasmo Leiva-Merikakis (San Francisco: Ignatius Press, 1982), 18–19.

4. Pope John Paul II, Letter to Artists, Vatican City: Libreria Editrice Vaticana, (4 April 1999): 38.

5. Dietrich von Hildebrand, "Beauty in the Light of the Redemption," *Logos* (Spring, 2001): 88–89.

6. Balthasar, *Love Alone Is Credible*, trans. D. C. Schindler (San Francisco: Ignatius Press, 2004), 23.

7. Edward T. Oakes, SJ, and David Moss, *The Cambridge Companion to Hans Urs von Balthasar* (Cambridge: Cambridge University Press, 2004), 270.

8. Cihak, 4.

9. In his poem "Archaic Torso of Apollo," Ranier Maria Rilke writes, "You must change your life."

10. Thiessen, 6.

11. Quoted in Regis Martin, *The Last Things: Death, Judgment, Heaven, Hell* (San Francisco: Ignatius Press, 1998), 39.

12. John Henry Newman, *Heart of Newman* (London: Sheed & Ward, 1930), 298–299.

4.

HOLY MASS AS HEAVEN ON EARTH

Then I looked, and I heard the voice of many angels surrounding the throne and the living creatures and the elders; they numbered myriads of myriads and thousands of thousands, singing with full voice,

"Worthy is the Lamb that was slaughtered
to receive power and wealth and wisdom and might
and honor and glory and blessing!"

Then I heard every creature in heaven and on earth and under the earth and in the sea, and all that is in them, singing,

"To the one seated on the throne and to the Lamb
be blessing and honor and glory and might
forever and ever!"

—REVELATION 5:11-13

In the presence of angels I sing to you,
I bow down before your holy Temple.

—PSALM 138:1-2 (NJB)

In the Eucharist, wrote St. Ignatius of Antioch, we "break the one bread that provides the medicine of immortality, the antidote for death and the food that makes us live forever in Jesus Christ."[1] The Church teaches that "the Kingdom of God has been coming since the Last Supper, and in the Eucharist, it is in our midst."[2]

Nowhere on earth are we visited more concretely by heaven than in the Holy Mass.

SINGING WITH ANGELS

It's embarrassing to admit this, but I never really thought specifically about the Mass and heaven until I was thirty years old. One day at noon Mass, where we didn't even sing the *Holy, Holy*, I was struck by the phrase, "And so with all the choirs of angels we proclaim your glory and join in their unending hymn of praise." I had heard it thousands of times, but for whatever reason, on that day, it registered.

I straightened up right then and thought, "I'm singing with angels!" I wanted to turn around to the ten or twelve others who were there for Mass that day and say, "We're singing with angels, choirs of angels. Right now! Did you know that?" I don't even remember reciting the *Holy, Holy* during that Mass, so struck was I by this notion. As I recall, the priest waited for me to kneel down with the others to begin the Eucharistic prayer; I was still half standing, suspended in my stupor even after all the rest of the congregation had completed the final "Hosanna, in the highest." As I said, it was a little embarrassing.

But looking around at the others gathered there, even those devoted ones who never missed daily Mass, even those who thoroughly embraced the real presence of Jesus in his body and blood, soul and divinity, I am guessing that the reality of joining the choir of heavenly hosts was quite far from their thoughts. To be sure, the presence of the Savior is far more awesome than his heavenly court, but there was something very pragmatic and useful about realizing that I was lifting my voice with angelic beings in praise of the Holy One. It suddenly made the glories of heaven more real and the rough patches of earth a little less lonely.

This reality is rarely lost on me now. Whether we sing or recite the *Holy, Holy* in Mass, I lift my voice and heart and eyes and see the heavenly hosts with all the saints in my imagination. They are crowded around the altar, hanging from the church rafters, squeezing in between altar servers and lectors and human choirs, clamoring politely, as angels and saints would, eager to witness the most spectacular moment of heaven on earth: "This is my body, given up for you."

And when I sing the *Holy, Holy*, I open my mouth and *sing*. No matter that my once-seasoned alto now strains to hit the high notes. No matter that those around me may not join in my enthusiasm. It is a fact that I am in concert with heavenly hosts, angels in heaven who behold the face of God, angels who worship the Holy One, singing right *now*, "Worthy is the Lamb." How glorious! I'm singing with angels—and so are you.

It hardly ends there. "The Mass," writes Bible scholar Scott Hahn, "and I mean *every* single Mass—is heaven on earth."[3] This isn't some thin metaphor grown stale with overuse. It is real. But what does it mean? How—on earth—is that possible?

ONE WORSHIP

There wasn't always this great, misty veil between heaven and earth. We recall that in the garden, Adam and Eve enjoyed perfect communion with God, until disobedience and pride swelled and consequences followed. After the fall, it was not only man who suffered separation from God, the entire earth was torn away from heaven as well. The Mass is the most poignant, most powerful place—and *powerful* doesn't even begin to capture the breadth of its strength—where heaven and earth are reunited in a palpable way. In the Mass, eternal divinity and human temporality keep close company once again. "This is what was unveiled in the Book of Revelation," writes Hahn, "the union of heaven and earth, consummated in the Holy Eucharist."[4]

We began by reflecting on the universal human longing for heaven and how heaven was impressed on the heart of every human being. In *The Lamb's Supper: The Mass as Heaven on Earth*, Hahn reads the Mass with eschatological eyes; he reads it through the lens of the Book of Revelation and identifies another important universal human experience. He notes, "For within the Apocalypse emerges a pattern—of covenant, fall, judgment, and redemption—and this pattern does describe a particular period of history, but it also describes *every* period of history, and *all* of history, as well as the course of life for each and every one of us."[5]

This notion is key when we begin to think about heaven, when we try to practice an eternal perspective and make heaven a habit of daily life. *We* are the stories, the characters of Scripture. We are the thief on the cross and Mary Magdalene and the Good Samaritan. We are King David and the roaming Israelites. We live out the same patterns of fall and redemption, and we are on the same great adventure toward either heaven or hell. Salvation history is our history; it is our past, our present, our future, and more.

In the same way that we might read Scripture by inserting ourselves into each story and each parable in order to better understand it, we also need to insert ourselves into heaven in order to understand its work: to worship God in the fullness of his glory. The Mass makes this insertion not only an exercise of the imagination, but a reality. Hahn observes that

> according to ancient Jewish beliefs, the worship in Jerusalem's Temple mirrored the worship of the angels in heaven. The levitical priesthood, the covenant liturgy, the sacrifices served as shadowy representations of heavenly models.
>
> Still, the Book of Revelation was up to something different, something more. Whereas Israel prayed *in imitation of the angels*, the Church of the Apocalypse worshiped *together with the angels* (see Revelation 19:10). Whereas only the priests were allowed in the holy place of Jerusalem's Temple, Revelation showed a nation of priests (see 5:10; 20:6) dwelling always in the presence of God.
>
> No longer would there be a heavenly archetype and an earthly imitation. Revelation now revealed *one worship*, shared by men and angels![6]

Did you catch that? One revealed worship, not to be imitated, but to be *shared*. (We're singing with angels again!) Jesus makes it possible for us to join in the work of heaven while still very much on earth, and heaven's holy and joyous business is worship. It is a perpetual delight in the glory of God. That is the plan, the master plan of the Master Planner. This is the Mass.

ALL OF THE GRACE OF HEAVEN

The Mass is heaven on earth. It has to be. God does not abandon or destroy his creation; he redeems it. And without access to the atonement, we are in trouble. Without the Eucharist, heaven is lost to us. We need its grace to fight the good fight that remains for those of us on earth—you and me. Heaven wants to see us win; heaven knows, the battle for truth, goodness, and beauty is real, and we need the weaponry—heaven itself—that is given to us in each Mass.

Revelation reminds us that

war broke out in heaven; Michael and his angels fought against the dragon. The dragon and his angels fought back, but they were defeated, and there was no longer any place for them in heaven. The great dragon was thrown down, that ancient serpent, who is called the Devil and Satan, the deceiver of the whole world—he was thrown down to the earth, and his angels were thrown down with him. . . . Then the dragon was angry with the woman, and went off to make war on the rest of her children, those who keep the commandments of God and hold the testimony of Jesus. (Revelation 12:7-9, 17)

If you keep the commandments, you are a part of the war. If you give testimony, calling yourself a Christian, you are under attack. Hahn describes it this way:

> The beastly message is this: we are fighting spiritual forces: immense, depraved, malevolent forces. If we had to fight them alone, we'd be trounced . . . the solution has to match the problem, spiritual force for spiritual force, immense beauty for immense ugliness, holiness for depravity, love for malevolence. The solution is the Mass, when heaven touches down to save an earth under siege.[7]

No one is suggesting that you start looking for Satan lurking behind every bush. But neither should we cast him off as an optional belief. Satan's greatest weapon is convincing you he doesn't exist. What is important is not focusing on that ancient deceiver, but focusing on the Savior. We don't dwell on the bloody battlefield of evil; we linger over the blood of the Lamb and remember, as Hahn writes, that "the grace available in the Mass is infinite—it's all the grace of heaven. The only limit is our capacity to receive it."[8]

All the grace of heaven: keep that phrase close to your heart the next time you step across a church threshold for Mass; keep it handy the next time you are tempted to despair. Keep it near you, in your breast pocket, when fear threatens to block the lifeblood of the eternal perspective from flooding the chambers of your heart.

READY TO RECEIVE

A small heart can receive small graces; a huge heart, on the other hand, can take in huge amounts of grace and, therefore, manifest more of heaven on earth. So, how does one achieve huge-heartedness?

I have a dear girlfriend who has four young daughters. I lived with her and her family for a time after she'd had her fourth child and helped to take care of her girls. One day when they were being especially naughty and quarrelsome, fighting in the backseat of the minivan over ownership of a ratty doll, I saw a subdued disappointment cross my friend's face. Something about her expression seemed deeper than the normal amount of frustration any parent of small children might have in a similar circumstance, and it made me curious.

She disciplined the girls and the day went on, but I asked her later what she'd been thinking in that moment. I'll never forget her response.

She explained that she'd been planning to take the girls for ice cream as a surprise all day long. "Not for any reason," she said, "but just because I love them." But when they started fighting over that doll, she could see that they were in no condition to be rewarded. It made her sad because she couldn't give them this treat that she had planned. She said, "It made me think, God must be like that with us. He has so many wonderful graces to pour out on us, but our disobedience prevents it. Instead we argue over dilapidated dolls. We miss out, and we don't even know it.

Disobedience can just make us so . . ." and here she stammered for just a moment before landing on *"clueless."*

The graces of Mass are not like ice cream at the end of the day but are more abundant than we even know, more than we expect, more than we can see from our point of view in the backseat, *more*, just because God loves us. And sometimes, we miss them entirely.

So often we too are "clueless" at Mass. We can get distracted, our minds may wander, and we may even begrudge the fact that we have to get up and out of the house on Sunday morning. We may tramp in late and inappropriately dressed, avoid reconciliation and receive the Eucharist unworthily, as though it were just a bit of bread. We go through the motions and miss the Mass entirely. We settle for arguments over dilapidated dolls, and because our hands are clutching busily and greedily to the earth, they are not free and open to receive the gifts our Father has planned for us. We miss "all the grace of heaven." We miss heaven on earth.

PROTECT US FROM ALL ANXIETY

Sometimes our cluelessness is obvious and self-inflicted; selfishness or pride or distractions tempt us to wander away from heaven. But sometimes, the enemy is far more subtle and insidious.

After I finished graduate school for the first time, I experienced some strange and alarming symptoms that no one could accurately diagnose. I went to doctor after doctor who ran test after test. MRIs and blood work were ordered. Internists consulted with neurologists who consulted with otolaryngologists and a whole tribe of other "ists." They rapped my knees to test my reflexes and stuck needles into my eardrum to measure the pressure. I went to naturopaths and chiropractors and began a rigorous vegan diet, then a "yeast-free" plan of eating. I tried acupuncture and massage, but nothing seemed to help.

I was casually handed numerous diagnoses, from "it might be a brain tumor" to "you have multiple sclerosis" to "it's nothing; you just need a vacation." This went on for months and months, and to this day has never been resolved entirely. The low point came when the original doctor I consulted said, "Well, I can't find anything wrong with you. Maybe you do have MS and we just haven't caught it yet." And with that, he sent me out of his office.

I was terrified. I had a relative and several friends who suffered from multiple sclerosis; I was familiar with how difficult it could be to diagnose as well as its unpredictable, creeping devastation, like dominoes falling in slow motion. It seemed all that was left to do was to sit and await the relentless onslaught of this progressively disabling disease. There has been far too much fear in my life as a general rule, but this particular circumstance stands out among the most terrifying episodes.

The uncertainty and the "not knowing" were excruciating; I was paralyzed with fear—of future paralysis. Friends encouraged me, my parents prayed unceasingly and helped with doctor bills, my employer understood when I missed work, but I was a wreck, failing miserably on the "do not be afraid" assignment. I felt utterly doomed.

There was only one place where my fear seemed to ebb, even if only for a moment: in the presence of the Eucharist, either at

Mass or in adoration. And in those fear-filled days, one petition among all those recited throughout the Mass jumped to the surface of my awareness like a beacon announcing the safety of shore on a stormy night at sea. Lodged between the Our Father and the Sign of Peace, the priest prays: *Protect us from every anxiety as we wait in joyful hope for the coming of our Savior, Jesus Christ.*

The first time the prayer really took hold in my mind, I thought, how impossible! To wait in joyful hope of the second coming and the promise of heaven, when all I could imagine was an abbreviated, stunted life punctuated with wheelchairs, increasing immobility, and isolation? The prayer felt ridiculous to me, and my faith was as feeble and fragile as my body. But then, instinctively, I started to cling to the first half of the prayer: *Protect us from all anxiety*. It was a beginning, a place to start, and intrinsically I knew it was answered already in eternity. I wouldn't have articulated it then, but I have come to understand that this is part of heaven's holy work here on earth—to protect us from fear—and the Mass embodies this work most perfectly.

Fear, anxiety, sin: these things cannot exist in heaven. In as much as I was able to receive the heavenly graces available to me through the Mass, my fear was relieved. It made perfect metaphysical sense. Even with my faith like a shriveled mustard seed, I was palpably protected from *all anxiety*—fear of illness, which, like all fear, was really fear of the future[9]—and because the Mass orients us more accurately, it recalibrates our perspective toward heaven. It holds up the atonement, which infuses all time, all space, all understanding. In the Eucharist, heaven reaches its holy arms around the earth and envelops it whole in a loving, perfecting embrace. In the Mass, through the Eucharist, we are literally able to step outside of time and into the timelessness of eternity. And there is simply no fear there. The Mass is where our two assignments meet and become one: we are not afraid *because* we have grasped an eternal perspective, or rather, it has grasped us.

TIME IN ETERNITY

You might think of it this way. Expanding on an idea from Peter Kreeft's *Heaven: The Heart's Deepest Longing*, we may imagine time as a straight line extending from the point of creation into infinity. Time has a starting point, like the eraser at the top of a pencil, and continues, like the line of the pencil down toward the tip of the lead and beyond. Time began at creation (the eraser), and somewhere on that line (along the body of the pencil), you were conceived and joined in time's trajectory into the future.

All material things are tied to time; all material things, including human beings, experience "before" and "after." But God exists outside of time and all time is present to God. There is no "before" for God, no "after." The philosophers teach us that God has no potential; the perfect act of God is God. By this we mean that there's no potential for God to become greater or better or more or change in any way somewhere in the future. He is perfect, immutable, omniscient, and omnipresent. All creation, including all time, is completely and always available to God; only God is eternal. Human souls are immortal, but they have a beginning point, a point of creation. God has no beginning, no end. God is.

Now, take that same pencil and turn it toward you until you are seeing it end-on, so that it becomes a point instead of a line. The Eucharist is this point, and it extends through and infuses every point on the line of time, backwards and forwards. The incarnation, when eternal divinity entered human temporality, is this point. The Last Supper is this point, along with Calvary, infusing every point on the line. Easter morning, a fiery pink sun rising on the horizon, slipping its rays of light across a hopeless, darkened landscape to find an empty tomb: this is also the point, infusing the whole line of time, and every single moment of your life—past, present, and future.

Heaven's perspective sees the point. It sees all of time, all at once, and is therefore able to redeem it. Many of the saints understood this reality, including St. Teresa of Ávila who even composed a prayer: "To Redeem Lost Time."[10] "[Eternity] is transcendent," writes Kreeft, "but it is also immanent in the whole line; in fact, it *is* the whole line looked at end-on. . . . Only eternity sees time as a whole."[11] And it is critical that we understand this when we go to Mass or make a holy hour.

We kneel before the one atonement of Calvary—once for all, for eternity—at every single Mass. There's no additional sacrifice. It's not a "repeat performance" of the Last Supper; Christ does not die again and again. The sacrifice we witness, with all the angels and saints at every Mass, is *the* sacrifice. Each Mass turns the line of time to face us as a single, unified point; and every fear and sorrow and problem you face—every happiness and joy— is swallowed up into that point of heavenly glory, and perfected. We remember that by his cross and resurrection, we have been set free, free from the bondage of our temporality, free from death, free from time, and free from fear. Repeat this to yourself: *By your cross and resurrection, Lord, I have been set free from fear*. It is a metaphysical, supernatural reality.

The Holy Mass is not a spiritual time machine transporting us to a different time in history. Rather, the Mass makes it possible for us to step off the line of time and enter into the point of eternity, into heaven's perspective, into heaven. The Mass is the place where heaven *and* earth are full of his glory. It insists on the incarnation, the marriage of human and divine, the perfect intermingling of temporal and eternal. Its beauty, embodied in the precious body and blood held high at every Mass, is strewn lavishly across human history, hovering over us in perpetuity. There will always be those who refuse it, like someone standing with his back to the morning sun, feeling its warmth and light and the promise of the day ahead, while denying the very shadow cast out before him. Don't be one of these. Step out of time and step into the Mass, into the warmth and glory of the Son.

THE SONG OF HEAVEN AND THE WHOLE WORLD

To be sure, it is important to reflect on the Holy Mass from the perspective of theologians and philosophers. While Church teaching on such matters is never set aside, it can also be helpful to hear from those who burst through the Church's doors because they have simply fallen wildly in love with the liturgy. One of my favorites is English author and artist Caryll Houselander.

In speaking of the Mass, she once wrote in a journal, "How sweet it is that we are permitted to live in Heaven." Houselander, who had been baptized as a baby, had a sporadic formation as a Catholic. She officially entered the Church as a young woman in 1925, drawn first and last by the liturgy. Her description of the Mass is particularly astute, in part because her converted eyes were fresh for the experience and in part because she was a true artist. Her words show an uncanny, poetic affinity for seeing in the Mass the whole of heaven *and* human experience. She writes,

> The supreme expression on earth of the rhythmic law of God is the Liturgy; . . . [it] expresses every passion, every emotion, every experience of the human heart. It is the song of the whole world; but it is also much more: it is the love-song of Christ in man, the voice of the Mystical Body of Christ lifted up to God. All our inarticulate longing and adoration, all our stammered incoherent love, set in tremendous metre of the Liturgy and lifted on the voice of Christ to our Heavenly Father.
>
> All those things which manifest the beauty of the Law are integrated in the Liturgy: music, poetry, rhythm.
>
> The slow majestic movements of the celebrant at the altar, the great sign of the cross, the deep obeisance, the lifting up and wide spreading of the arms—all ordered, measured, disciplined, to be the medium of Christ's adoration.
>
> The words, new on the priest's tongue at every Mass, are the words that have worn deep grooves in the human mind through the ages, like the river-beds worn in the rocks.[12]

We know them by heart, those river-bed words, even more deeply than we think, perhaps more deeply than we dare. They have been worn into us by a river of love. In the raising of the host, then the cup, heaven comes to join us in "the song of the whole world": *This is my Body, given up for you.* Then we all sing, men and angels, heaven and earth, the eternal tune, "the love-song of Christ."

1. James O'Connor, *The Hidden Manna: A Theology of the Eucharist* (San Francisco: Ignatius Press, 1988), 141, 206ff.

2. *Catechism of the Catholic Church* (Vatican City: Libreria Editrice Vaticana, 1997), 2816.

3. Scott Hahn, *The Lamb's Supper: The Holy Mass as Heaven on Earth* (New York: Doubleday, 1999), 5.

4. Hahn, 125.

5. Hahn, 73.

6. Hahn, 69–70.

7. Hahn, 85.

8. Hahn, 161.

9. Kreeft writes, "Time is the condition for all fear; that's why time is the enemy. For fear is always of the future, fear of what might happen next, not of what is actually happening now. Some psychologists think as much as nine-tenths of pain is mental, not physical, induced by fear and removable by fearlessness." Peter Kreeft, *Heaven: The Heart's Deepest Longing* (San Francisco: Ignatius Press, 1989).

10. "O My God! Source of all mercy! I acknowledge Your sovereign power. While recalling the wasted years that are past, I believe that You, Lord, can in an instant turn this loss to gain. Miserable as I am, yet I firmly believe that You can do all things. Please restore to me the time lost, giving me Your grace, both now and in the future, that I

may appear before You in 'wedding garments.' Amen." *Prayers and Heavenly Promises* (Rockford, IL: Tan Books and Publishers, 1990), 105.

11. Kreeft, 86.

12. Caryll Houselander, *The Passion of the Infant Christ* (New York: Sheed & Ward, 1949), 35–36.

5.

THE INHABITANTS OF HEAVEN

Holy Mary, Mother of God . . . pray for us.
Our Lady of Grace . . . pray for us.
Our Lady of Perpetual Help . . . pray for us.
Our Lady of Guadalupe . . . pray for us.
St. Michael . . . pray for us.
St. Gabriel . . . pray for us.
St. Raphael . . . pray for us.
Holy Angels of God . . . pray for us.
St. John the Baptist . . . pray for us.
St. Joseph . . . pray for us.
St. Joseph of Cupertino . . . pray for us.
St. Peter and St. Paul . . . pray for us.
St. Andrew, St. John, and St. James . . . pray for us.
St. Thomas and St. Mark . . . pray for us.
St. Anne, mother of Mary . . . pray for us.
St. Mary Magdalene . . . pray for us.
St. Stephen . . . pray for us.
St. Ignatius of Antioch . . . pray for us.
St. Agnes . . . pray for us.
St. Agatha . . . pray for us.
St. Augustine . . . pray for us.
St. Thomas Aquinas . . . pray for us.
St. Benedict . . . pray for us.
St. Gertrude . . . pray for us.

St. Lucy . . . pray for us.
St. Joan of Arc . . . pray for us.
St. Elizabeth of the Trinity . . . pray for us.
St. Catherine of Siena . . . pray for us.
St. Pio . . . pray for us.
St. John of the Cross . . . pray for us.
St. Teresa of Ávila . . . pray for us.
St. Maximilian Kolbe . . . pray for us.
St. Thérèse of Lisieux . . . pray for us.
St. Maria Goretti . . . pray for us.
Blessed Mother Teresa . . . pray for us.
All holy men and women . . . pray for us.

Heaven won't be lonely. Happily, it might even be a touch on the crowded side. As Jesus said, his Father's house has many rooms (see John 14:2).

We have reflected on heaven as our true and eternal home, as revealed in beauties of the earth and each other, free from all fear, and as ultimately glorious, filled with perpetual praise of the Holy One. It is a further delight to understand that we will experience none of these things alone. In addition to enjoying loving communion with God, we will also enjoy a loving community of other immortal creatures, the inhabitants of heaven: the saints, the angels, and the Blessed Mother. It is important to remember that we do not get to heaven on our own; we get there as a Church.

The Christian life is a terrifically rich and interesting one, and if you ever doubt it, you need only ponder for a moment this communal aspect of heaven. We believe, according to the *Catechism of the Catholic Church*, that "heaven is the blessed community of all who are perfectly incorporated into Christ,"[1] and that "in the glory of heaven the blessed continue joyfully to fulfill God's will in relation to other men and to all creation."[2] What a thrilling notion, that death is no barrier between the blessed in heaven or on earth. We continue to interact with one another, working together toward the fulfillment of the Father's will from wherever we are in eternity.

This notion is made even more intriguing by the miraculous fact that, sometimes, these beings of heaven enter into our company on earth in ways we can perceive with our senses—in apparitions, visions, interior locutions, and the like. In a marvelous scene in Willa Cather's novel *Death Comes for the Archbishop*, one of the characters, a priest, speaking about the apparition of Our Lady of Guadalupe, says, "Where there is great love there are always miracles . . . One might almost say that an apparition is human vision corrected by divine love . . . The Miracles of the Church seem to me to rest not so much upon faces or voices or healing power coming suddenly near to us from afar off, but upon our perceptions being made finer, so that for a moment our eyes can see and our ears can hear what is there about us always."

Heaven is "about us always," whether we see it or not. And we will find the truest community there, a community of friendship, intercession, protection, guidance, encouragement, and love that does not fail. But until our hoped-for entrance into Zion, heaven has seen fit to allow the saints and angels and Mary to appear to us in one way or another. For, often it seems that when our trust has run out, when our faith has worn too thin, we need to borrow the faith of others—faith that is greater than ours, faith that has been perfected in paradise.

Saints and angels and Our Lady of Grace, pray for us.

THE COMMUNION OF SAINTS

His name is Joseph, and he is one of the greatest lovers I've ever known. We first became acquainted when I was in my twenties, still so full of that youthful passion that is bent on finding new loves. Of course, Joseph had been dead for centuries, but this was not the slightest obstacle to our becoming close. He is my most highly favored saint, Joseph of Cupertino.

Young Joseph, born in the Italian village of Cupertino (Copertino) in 1603, had a rough start. His father died before he was born, leaving behind debts that his mother could not repay. She lost everything, including their home; Joseph was born in a shed behind the house.

Unfortunately, Joseph's relationship with his mother left much to be desired. She is said to have blamed Joseph for her husband's death. Strict to the point of being abusive, she eventually rejected Joseph altogether. Ironically, it did not help matters that Joseph was given rare spiritual gifts even from childhood, visions and ecstasies that literally took him to heaven. He was given the nickname "the Gaper" for wandering around with his mouth open, as if he were in a trance.

Joseph was unusually absentminded and clumsy, and when it came time for him to apprentice, he was simply unable to learn any craft. He failed at shoemaking, even dishwashing. His increasingly frequent ecstasies left him completely unsuited for the routine demands of commonplace labors. Between the harshness of his home life and the frustration he must have felt over his failures in the workplace, he developed a raging temper. At seventeen he tried to enter a religious order but was rejected for his lack of schooling and what might be diagnosed today as a learning disability. His own mother regarded him as "good for nothing."

Ouch. As I said, off to a rough start.

Then a relative who was living as a member of a religious order intervened on Joseph's behalf. Joseph was given a tertiary habit and assigned work in the stables of a Franciscan convent. There conversion truly took hold of him. Working among gentle barnyard beasts, his raging temper left him, and he began to grow dramatically in humility, holiness, and obedience while practicing great mortifications. I think this must have calmed his mind, too, for he was finally able, little by little, to study and retain small amounts of information necessary for test-taking. Thus, he began his formation for the priesthood.

According to one famous story, while preparing for a particular test, St. Joseph was only able to study one exam question. He prayed that the test would cover the material he knew. When it came time for the test, Joseph's superior asked the one question for which he had prepared well. He has since become the patron saint of students. But this was not the most remarkable aspect of Joseph's life.

Many saints in Church history have levitated, but none so often as St. Joseph. It has been recorded that he levitated on more than seventy occasions, winning him a new nickname, "the Flying

Fria." Soon, healings and other miracles would be associated with his prayers of intercession. He would fall into ecstasies at the mention of the name of Jesus. The sight of a lamb would bring the presence of the Lamb of God so close, so strongly to him, that he simply could not contain his joy. The law of love, which increasingly ruled his life, overruled the very law of gravity, eliminating any possible veil between heaven and earth. He saw, with reckless innocence, the one created reality of heaven and earth and the loving Creator who made it, and it was this absolute, joyful abandon that captured my devotion. Something in that convent stable—perhaps it was the simple work or, maybe, the constant reminder of the humble earthly beginnings of the Savior—vaulted Joseph beyond any barrier that might have stood between him and God. The filters dropped even further away until only holy joy was left. He was truly living—and flying—in the beatific vision.

Though he did not manage this perfectly, much of St. Joseph's life was marked by this "filter-free" living. Moment by moment, he was uniquely able to avail himself completely to God. There simply was no separation between his heart and God's presence. His ecstasies and raptures and moments of flight were dictated only by his finely tuned, heavenly perception. Still, a saint's life is never easy. The demands of heavenly assignments, while joyful, are often also painful. And sometimes they attract unwanted attention.

One day hell reached up and tried to choke the joy right out of Joseph. It tried to shackle him to itself, literally keep his feet—and heart—on the ground. As news of the extraordinary aspects of his faith life became better known, he came under the scrutiny of not only the curious but critics as well. He suffered persecution at the hands of other priests and religious who were so weighed down with every kind of worldly fear that this gentle, flying friar and his divine joy were simply too great a threat—a threat perhaps to their very manageable, predictable, containable unhappiness. He suffered years of imposed isolation where he was forbidden contact with others. This naturally resulted in aridity in his prayer life, even depression, as those false filters crept back to darken and subdue. Many pray to St. Joseph of Cupertino when they need to study or concentrate, but St. Joseph feels especially close to me when I feel rejected, isolated, alone, or forgotten. It is to address these difficulties that I most often call on his intercession.

On August 10, 1663, Joseph became deathly ill with a fever. In keeping with his nature, he was thrilled; soon he'd be in heaven! On the feast of the Assumption, just five days later, he levitated one final time during Mass. He died September 18 and is buried near St. Francis in Osimo, Italy. His funeral was attended by crowds of the faithful.

This is what the saints do: they embody the exhortations of Pope John Paul II to live beyond fear, to "live with an eternal perspective," sometimes in extraordinary and, at other times, very pragmatic ways. St. Joseph of Cupertino is but one example.

By their example, we come to learn that there is really only one great, distinguishing factor between us and them. Their love for our shared heavenly Father is so great that it renders the veil between heaven and earth sheer to nearly invisible, and this animates their lives with heavenly delight. From the world's perspective, they might appear ugly, odd, or even insane, but from heaven, oh, how they glow! Saints burn with such brilliant holy love that they light the whole world.

Chesterton wrote,

> The saint is a medicine because he is an antidote. Indeed that is why the saint is often a martyr; he is mistaken for a poison because he is an antidote. He will generally be found restoring the world to sanity by exaggerating whatever the world neglects; . . . he is not what the people want but rather what the people need. This is surely the very much mistaken meaning of those words to the first saints, "Ye are the salt of the earth." Salt seasons and preserves beef, not because it is like beef; but because it is very unlike it.[3]

We walk around in our world with a million and one filters that block the splendor of heaven, and a menagerie of fears that nag and peck relentlessly at our belief and our willingness to be salt, to be very unlike beef. These fears hinder heaven's love and crush joy fed from eternity. Which ones are operating in your world, keeping you from heavenly joy? Do any of these thoughts sound familiar? *What will people think? Is this all right? What will this require of me? Will I be okay? I'm no saint. It's too hard, too demanding, too expensive, too freakish, too impractical to think, to act, to be like a saint. I cannot—will not—become a saint.* But if you're a Christian, do you really have any other options? We are antidote or poison. Citizenship in heaven necessitates our sanctity, our eventual sainthood. St. Joseph had plenty of reasons to languish in bitterness or anger, in jealousy or sloth or entitlement, but somehow he managed it: sainthood. What's my excuse? What am I choosing? What are you choosing?

Deciding for Sanctity

Sainthood does not demand a PhD in sanctity; it demands a decision. You can choose, right now, to be an antidote, to live a life which embodies and even *exaggerates*, as Chesterton says, what the world neglects. Do you wish to draw heaven to earth? Do you want to be a saintly antidote? You need only look around and ask yourself, "What does my world neglect? What does it need?"

If we are to make a study of eternal life as Christians, we must examine the lives of the saints. The encyclopedia of saints that our Church professes provides a patron saint for every need, a teacher for every spiritual lesson. Find yourself a complete copy of one of the litanies, perhaps from All Saints Day, and recite it often. Learn the stories of the lives of those on the list. Their lives are vivid examples of the way in which we should go to prepare ourselves for paradise. Look to them; see their individual versions of spiritual antidote. Go to them with confidence and ask their intercession. They are experts in virtue. When the world tries to crush your eternal ambitions, you can trust that the saints are here, right now, present and available to help restore you to the absolute sanity of heavenly joy.

St. Maximilian Kolbe, for example, looked around and saw that his world was in desperate need of courage. He *exaggerated* courage, giving up his life in place of another in that desolate Nazi death camp. Blessed Mother Teresa *exaggerated* care for the poorest of the poor. St. Pio *exaggerated* our need for repentance. St. Thérèse of Lisieux *exaggerated* our need for "the little way." St. Teresa of Ávila *exaggerated* our need for holy imagination and deeper prayer. St. Elizabeth of Hungary *exaggerated* our need for generosity. St. Elizabeth of the Trinity *exaggerated* our need to embrace the mystery of our triune God. St. Augustine *exaggerated* our need for clarity in doctrine. The apostles and martyrs *exaggerated to death* our need for the truth. The list is endless. If your name is to be added, what will the world accuse you of exaggerating?

What lives like this reveal is astonishing. We get this backwards sometimes, but saints are not *self*-conscious, they are *God*-conscious. (St. Joseph was so God-conscious he literally could not keep his feet on the ground!) Saints do not dwell in unhealthy shame over their own sinfulness and failings. Instead saints are filled with humility and deep gratitude because they recognize the great love and mercy of the Father to use them despite their sinfulness. Armed with this recognition, they fight the good fight aimed at eternity, not because they think *nothing* of themselves but because they think *everything* and *all the time* of God. St. John of the Cross would say, "Think of nothing but God's providence." Ultimately, all saints exaggerate eternity and the love of God.

St. Paul exhorts us this way: "Fight the good fight of the faith; take hold of the eternal life, to which you were called and for which you made the good confession in the presence of many witnesses" (1 Timothy 6:12). He goes on to remind us that it is "the King of kings and Lord of lords . . . he alone who has immortality and dwells in unapproachable light, whom no one has ever seen or can see; to him be honor and eternal dominion" (1 Timothy 6:15-16). Reflecting on this passage, Balthasar writes,

> What counts is to hang on to what has been chosen and thereby to "take firm hold on everlasting life" by anticipation. Persistence in this choice will require constant struggle, and "the good fight of faith" must be carried on "without blame or reproach" as an assignment from Christ and the Church. Yet to "take hold of everlasting life" does not mean grabbing at God. . . . The God "who dwells in unapproachable light, whom no man has ever seen or can see," can only be worshiped, never grasped by men. To decide for God, to bear witness to him, means just the opposite: to be grasped by him and placed under assignment.[4]

The saints understand this truth. While on earth, they await their marching orders with little or no hesitation. In love, trust, and anticipation, they take hold of eternal life and in turn are taken up into the arms of the Father. Heaven moves in, sometimes like a tempest, sometimes like a gentle evening breeze, to blow back earth's veil and reveal God's glory.

In heaven, as on earth, the saintly assignment is to worship God by exaggerating, magnifying him, loving him "who dwells in unapproachable light," and the love that is generated from this eternal work overflows the banks of heaven's river and is poured out on us in unending intercession. Intercession simply cannot be helped; the second assignment springs from the first. The saint has ordered his life—"*ordinate in me caritatem*"[5]—and his obedience draws out heaven's response: superabundant, lavish love.

Saints have faced the fork in the road between "my will" or "thy will." Just like Jesus, they chose God's will, they chose heaven. Just like Jesus, saints are heroically obedient to the will of the Father, and just like Jesus, this meant death—death on a cross, death to self, death. Obedience meant that the cup would not pass, that scourge and cross would come, and that heavy bloodstained wood would claim his life.

Just at this point, we are tempted to stop, reconsider, take a step back. We may enjoy the thought of exaggeration; we're intrigued even to "fight the good fight." It's this bloody, painful death, this total giving of self we're not so sure we can fit into our busy, tidy schedule and our self-preserving hearts.

Balthasar reminds us that the apostles had to learn that "to glory in the Lord" would mean "to glory in the Cross of Christ." He writes, "The disciples who were listening to the Beatitudes would have to learn this gradually as they experienced Christ's Passion and Resurrection and the sending of the Holy Spirit."[6] Learning the road to sanctity for St. Joseph of Cupertino was a gradual one, and not particularly elegant or refined. It was a tumultuous, difficult business for St. Peter; he had to be turned around by the Lord himself: *Quo vadis?* (Where are you going?) Lessons came slow—"so late have I loved you"—for St. Augustine, too. And these were spiritual giants! It's neither so shocking nor off-putting, then, that our learning will be gradual, too. We'll have phases that are riddled with errors and failings of every kind. The point is to recognize that we learn the road, choose the road, and choose the road again and again when weariness or fear or selfishness or self-deception creeps up to lead us off course.

Most of us will never face a dramatic martyrdom. Most of us will never be physically tortured for our faith. Most of us will not experience extraordinary mystical gifts like levitation or bi-location, gifts that might make our lives a spectacle.

For most of us, heaven will be chosen in the often tiny day-to-day things: a kind word spoken and a cutting word withheld; money that might have been spent on a haircut given to the poor instead; taking an unexpected spare moment when you might have rested to pray for someone who is lonely; seeing what you have rather than what you lack; forgiving someone who has falsely accused you and then forgetting the offense altogether; sneaking away in the middle of the night to make a holy hour; playing one more game of Go Fish with your six-year-old nephew. It takes tremendous courage of heart to be invisible, the hidden saint, the saint no one sees.

Our martyrdoms may be hidden, but they are not ineffectual. Our sainthood may be silent on earth, but it is already making tender music in heaven. Our road to sanctity might seem drab and less interesting than another's, but the glorious destination is exactly the same. The communion of saints—from the mystical masters, to the Church doctors, to the anonymous souls we have yet to meet—know you; they know your road; they chose that same road before you; and they are cheering you on even from heaven's amphitheater. When you are tempted to point yourself in a hellish direction, you can turn to them with complete confidence because they are experts in intercession. They will perfect your prayer. They will ready your prayer for entrance into heaven, where it will be recorded before the Almighty.

WALKING ON HEAVEN

My first semester back in graduate school, I signed up for an hour of adoration in the middle of the night, each week on Tuesdays. A group of students had organized perpetual adoration on campus. There are few things that minister to me more than adoration in the quiet of the night, and I always looked forward to my chilly night walks to the chapel. As it turns out, one of the nights I was "on guard" was the feast of All Saints. After my hour was finished, I bundled up for the walk home and stepped out into the cold air.

As is typical of many university settings, the quad is criss-crossed by cement walking paths. But instead of being met with flat, white cement, my boots collided with heaven itself. Some students had taken sidewalk chalk and covered every path with the litany of the saints: "St. Augustine, pray for us! St. Joseph, pray for us! St. Pio, pray for us!" Under every step I took, a prayer issued, a prayer answered. It was palpable, such a perfect metaphor: literally and spiritually, walking on, upheld by the strength and prayers and devotion of the inhabitants of heaven. I felt light as a feather on that walk home, joy in the soles of my shoes.

And something about that long litany, that yellow brick road of sanctity, reminded me that, from an eternal perspective, there are saints already very much among us. They are our friends and neighbors. They are our fathers and mothers and sisters and brothers and babies, our neighbors, friends and enemies, our flesh and bone. And God willing, maybe some All Saints Day in the future, someone will be scrawling your name, or perhaps the name of someone you know, on the pavement with sure and certain confidence that your prayers will hold them up and guide their feet straight to heaven's door.

St. Joseph of Cupertino and all holy men and women, pray for us.

THE HEAVENLY HOSTS

It is a prayer for children, and for the childlike: "Angel of God, my guardian dear, / to whom God's love commits me here. / Ever this day be at my side, / to light, to guard, to rule, to guide."

One appeared to Mary—we know the story so well. He came to say, *The Lord is with you, blessed one.* And later, another would appear to startled shepherds to announce, *A savior has been born*; a whole host would join in the ensuing joy, *Gloria in excelsis.* When Abraham was about to sacrifice his son Isaac, his hand was stayed by one such as these. Another helped the stubborn Tobias find the love of his life. They were there to witness the empty tomb, and when Jesus was most weary, after so much fasting and prayer and then temptation from the devil, they came to him and ministered.

Angels do more than sing.

They are very much a part of created reality, and though angels generally fall into the category of "things unseen," which we profess in each recitation of the Nicene Creed, they do, on occasion, become visible, audible, or sensible to us. They are particularly prominent and wonderfully interesting citizens of heaven, and they seem to be always in the thick of things on earth, occupying most readily the spiritual space where heaven and earth commingle.

Like human beings, angels enjoy a variety of gifts, or heavenly assignments. Some do battle; others minister and heal; others guard and protect; still others intercede in prayer. All are given to praise of the Almighty. Like people, the heavenly hosts have intellect, will, and personality. Like us, their souls are immortal.

But because they are pure spirit, as Pope John Paul II writes, their knowledge of God is "incomparably more perfect than that of man . . . they see to the depths the greatness of infinite Being, of the first Truth, of the supreme Good."[7] This depth helps to define the twofold nature of their vocation in all things seen and unseen: "to praise God, to be always in God's presence," and "to help human beings, according to God's purposes."[8]

Most familiar to us are those named in Scripture, the archangels Michael, Gabriel, and Raphael. When "war broke out in heaven" (Revelation 12:7), it was Michael and his angels who defeated the ancient serpent of Revelation. This is why we pray, "St. Michael, defend us in battle; be our defense against the wickedness and snares of the devil." Gabriel must certainly be one of God's favorites. Not only was he appointed to announce the incarnation, but as he reminded the questioning Zechariah, he stands in the presence of God (see Luke 1:19). According to Scripture, Raphael stayed with us a long while, keeping Tobias company on his difficult journey and helping him find his wife, Sarah, who was "sensible, brave, and very beautiful" (Tobit 6:12). Raphael tells us, "When you and Sarah prayed, it was I who brought and read the record of your prayer before the glory of the Lord" (12:12).

In the years that I most ardently prayed for a good husband, the verses of Tobit, the words of St. Raphael, were my prayer: "For she was set apart for you before the world was made," and Tobias "loved her very much, and his heart was drawn to her" (6:18). Each prayer was being read and recorded before the Lord himself by one of these extraordinary creatures. What a remarkable exchange! How much it inspires us to make our prayers worthy, humble, and earnest when we practice seeing with our hearts the path that each of our prayers will take and the glorious creature that will carry them. How heavenly and heaven-sent is the act of prayer, angels standing in our stead before the throne of heaven, face to face with God, perfecting our prayers for us so that they are worthy. To bolster your confidence in angels and their mission, I recommend reading this adventure of journeys and love in its entirety in the Book of Tobit. It is a wonderful angel story.

But when considering angels and delighting in their presence among us, we need to exercise some caution and wisdom. It is in the "things unseen" category that we either tend toward infatuation or total disregard. Angels are one of the areas of our faith life that we either overemphasize or tidily compartmentalize. Neither stance is healthy or in keeping with Church teaching on the matter.

Angels were rather in vogue in recent years. Their statuary filled gift shops. We lacquered them on coffee mugs and printed them on stationery. Bookstores filled their shelves with intriguing titles on heaven's messengers, and this inordinate and sudden attention was not necessarily bad. This interest may have reflected a deeper hunger for heaven, but I also wonder if it might not have been just one more way of substituting creatures for the Creator. It's so much easier for us to deal with all things "less than" God. These days, the angel craze has subsided considerably, and perhaps the angels are relieved.

Then there are those of us who may want to leave angels and the ways that they engage this earth back in the apostolic age. Maybe angels were around to deliver the good news of the resurrection, maybe they were busily employed during the Old and New Testaments, but the likelihood that angels move among us today, to guard and protect, ministering to our wounded world, seems farfetched, even silly. And this particular posture toward angels isn't accurate either.

Cardinal John Henry Newman said it this way:

There have been ages of the world in which men have thought too much of angels . . . [and have] honored them so perversely as to forget the supreme worship due to Almighty God. This is the sin of a dark age. But the sin of what is called an educated age, such as our own, is just the reverse; to account slightly of them, or not at all; to ascribe all we see around us, not to their agency, but to certain assumed laws of nature.[9]

Keeping these things in mind, neither mocking nor marketing the heavenly hosts, neither replacing God nor rejecting angels offhand, let us attempt to fall somewhere faithfully on middle ground.

ANGELS AMONG US

We will begin with a story that beautifully inhabits this middle way, angels as sensed and seen through prayerful use of the imagination. I recount this story here, written by my friend and colleague, Vinita Hampton Wright, not only because I love her and trust her word, but because her angelic encounter teaches us so much about how heaven embraces and upholds the earth. She details her experience in *A Catalogue of Angels: The Heavenly, the Fallen, and the Holy Ones Among Us.*

It had been an especially painful and frightening time in her life. Her husband, Jim, was struggling with severe depression, rendering him so vulnerable that he requested Vinita's company during his sessions with a therapist. She writes that during his appointments, she would sit silently, listening, mainly trying to pray. She writes,

> A good friend of mine suggested that I come up with an image that would represent God's care, or some other concept that would help me, and then meditate on that image during Jim's therapy session.
>
> So at Jim's next appointment, I came up with something not very original. I imagined an angel standing behind my husband, hands clasped on Jim's shoulders while he talked with [the therapist]. I sat there and closed my eyes and thought of this image; this was my prayer that evening.
>
> In a little while though, the image took on a life of its own. It was [as] if my mind's eye had become a movie camera and

that camera abruptly backed up a few feet, and I saw that the angel was now standing behind my husband with arms raised, and with this angel, making a small circle around Jim, were four or five other angels, all with arms raised in petition for him.

Then, just as suddenly, the camera backed up again, much further, and what I saw made my heart pound and my throat catch. There were *circles and circles and circles of angels* surrounding my husband, concentric circles numbering hundreds, thousands of angels. And all of them had arms raised, sending prayers heavenward for him. . . .

That image—and I remember how golden and shining it was—helped me through a season that was frightening and full of pain. On that evening, within a few seconds, I had been given a glimpse of God's love, manifested in this overwhelming support of the heavenly hosts who, invisible though they are, remain with us through every battle, arms raised to God's great heavenly presence.[10]

Vinita, an author and an artist, stewards her creativity with great holiness and discipline, and these things may have helped facilitate her angelic vision. But her experience is also a good reminder that her "not very original" image was the entry point for heaven's greater and more accurate illumination: that when we are frightened, when life feels radically painful and the best we are capable of is our not very original prayers, not only are we not alone and not rejected for our lack of imagination, we are *surrounded* by heaven. There are heavenly creatures appointed by God encircling us at our most fragile hours, a veritable army with arms raised in the mighty prayers of holy soldiers at war. It's true that we join the heavenly hosts in their praise when we sing, *Hosanna in the highest.* But we mustn't forget that when we ask for help, this same heavenly host rushes down, turning the full force of its attentions toward us, joining us—circles and circles of angels—in our quiet, little, unoriginal prayers. It is their purpose to do so.

Angels take our modest attempts, our "not very original" prayers that stand hollow and awkward like fragile old skeletons, and breathe life into them, filling out muscle and sinew, the flesh of eternal things. Then they record them in heaven. This is how our Father in heaven has ordered the world. That day, Vinita was given heaven's eyes for a moment. Though she did not see angels with human eyes, she saw them with her spirit, and just like the graces that pour out upon us in the Mass—the "more" of the Mass that we sometimes miss—she was delighted and surprised, comforted and consoled. Her faith was met and matched and magnified in *circles and circles, hundreds and thousands,* so much more of the love of heaven coming to visit than she ever imagined.

Angels Ignored

At times it can be difficult to believe the "more" of heaven. It seems too good to be true. We need to tell each other our angel stories, not to sensationalize heaven but because we need frequent reminders of its immutability and power, its reality and love. When heaven touches earth in ways we can see and feel, the gifts and graces are so palpable that we might hold them in our hands, fresh and holy fruit ready to meet us in our hunger for eternal things.

There has been only one time in my life that I sensed what I believe was an angel. I'd been out for dinner with a man that I did not know very well. At the end of the evening, he walked me to my door. Just as we were about to reach it, I felt as though someone was suddenly in front of me, grabbing both of my arms, shaking me once firmly, saying, "Stop right now and tell him that he cannot come in. Do not let him in your house!" It happened in an instant, but the message was completely clear. It was so real to me that I stopped for a moment, startled. The man I was with asked me what was wrong. Embarrassed, I replied, "Nothing."

It was a bitter cold night. The air was still and taut with temperatures well below zero. He shivered a bit and said, "Well, come on then, I'm freezing." We proceeded into my house and before I even knew what was happening, he assaulted me.

I do not recount this story to cast a shadow of doom across this book for warnings unheeded. Rather, I hope it will cast an entirely different hue—one of hope and gratitude and awe at a heaven that loves us so much that it will pierce the human veil to rescue and warn and protect, even if it leaves the final judgment on these visitations up to us.

Looking back, I did not doubt the experience or the veracity of the warning, but I was afraid. And naïve. My dating experience had been extremely limited, and I didn't want to be "rude." What folly! What I missed in my eagerness to be loved and accepted in this world was how very much I was already loved and accepted in another—so much so that heaven reached down with both hands to guard and guide even me.

But mostly, I try to remember the faith of Mary at the annunciation, and her sliver of confusion. When Gabriel appeared and declared to this perplexed young girl that she would give birth to Jesus, her initial response reflected no doubt in God whatsoever, but rather a well-reasoned doubt in the reality of her circumstances. Her only question was, "How can this be?" And the angel replied, "The power of the Most High will overshadow you . . . for nothing will be impossible with God" (Luke 1:34-35, 37).

If there is one singular angelic message that our heaven-seeking hearts must cultivate and live out day by day on this earth, it is this: in the moment of our greatest surrender to Jesus, the Most High will overshadow us, making all the things of heaven possible on earth. *All things*—all miracles, all restoration and healing, all friendship, all forgiveness, all mercy, all beauty and glory and joy and justice. *All things*. This is what we really mean when we pray, "Your kingdom come, your will be done on earth as it is in heaven." *Bring your heaven to earth, dear Lord*. This is what comes when we surrender like Mary and say, "Here am I, the servant of the Lord; let it be with me according to your word" (Luke 1:38).

Then angels rush home to record the prayer before the Almighty and the multitudes rejoicing there.

GUARDIAN DEAR

In Exodus, the Lord sent angels to guard and protect his people, to go "in front of [them], to guard [them] on the way and to bring

[them] to the place" that God had prepared for them (23:20-23). Likewise, many of the mystics and saints have acknowledged specific angels sent to guard us personally, angel guardians appointed to protect and nurture one human life. St. Basil wrote that "Beside each believer stands an angel as protector and shepherd leading him to life."[11] How long has it been since you requested the aid of your angel guardian? Did you leave those prayers kneeling at the bedside of your childhood?

Imagine for a moment this heavenly creature, immortal and beautiful, one that enjoys the very company of God—this creature is devoted solely to you, appointed entirely to your well-being. This invisible inhabitant of heaven knows God so deeply that in comparison, the most profound human thoughts appear as the awkward babblings of a baby. This very angel is there with you now, ready to take your personal prayers and petitions, just like Tobit and Sarah kneeling at their bedside, straight to the seat of heaven. What love God must have for us, to give us—each one of us—such an unspeakably holy and powerful gift, tying us in a very real way to the daily workings of heaven itself.

On the day I was assaulted, I trust that I was not abandoned by heaven. No, my guardian angel was right there with me, and in that mystical way that angels and men meet, he broke through all that keeps me in bondage to this earth to touch me, to speak to me, to give me heaven's eyes for a moment. And I wonder how much it must have grieved him to see my innocence betrayed, how heavy was his spirit to know the devastating consequences— criminal, spiritual, and emotional—awaiting my attacker. How fervent must his prayers have been, arms raised heavenward, as the door closed shut behind me, locking out the startling reality of his visitation along with the bitter winter air.

There is always the chance that had I tried to send this man away from my house, he may have forced himself in anyway. I do not bother with, "If only . . ." Instead, the mystery, the terrible, holy truth I cling to with trembling hands in recalling that moment is that I was not alone. Angels were there, even more than I knew, circles and circles and circles, hundreds and thousands, and their prayers were rising like incense to an all-too-attentive heaven, a heaven that had plans for me, for my restoration, for a future with hope.

And those same heavenly hands that held my arms in their urgent grip would be the same hands of healing to come and live with me later on, ever faithful, immortal sentinels appointed by my Father to light, to guard, to rule, to guide. Even me.

Angels were there then. Angels are here now, *encircling, encircling*, arms and arms, such holy, mighty arms raised, raising, *just for you.*

St. Michael, St. Raphael, St. Gabriel, my angel guardians, pray for us.

QUEEN OF HEAVEN AND EARTH

My apartment is two blocks from the University of St. Thomas campus library. As a graduate student, I've grown very fond of the place, not only for its convenient location, its good lighting, and the undergraduates milling about with their youthful enthusiasm, but also because it remains open until 2:00 a.m. during the school year, a fact I relish as an undeniably nocturnal creature. Much of the writing I've done in the past few years has taken place there in the wee small hours of the morning.

I situate myself at a table on the third floor near the stacks that contain the art and art history holdings. My first ambition as a kid, after astronaut, was to become a painter. As a result, I studied painting and art history for many years. To sit in the company of these voluminous tomes dedicated to the world's greatest masters of art is a comfort, my own little late-night salon.

One day I happened to notice the Michelangelo collection. Among these works there was a particularly large and vivid book on his paintings and sculpture. I have become quite attached to it. Often, I will take it down from the shelf while I'm working and prop it up against the wall or a chair to keep me company. The front cover is a close-up photograph of the face of the Blessed Mother taken from Michelangelo's *Pietà*. (You will remember the work from our chapter on beauty.) The photo is taken in such a way that when I place the book at the right angle, this beautiful, young Madonna—her features so flawless—"looks on" as I work. She watches over me.

I feel a special intimacy with the Madonna. It is a comfort to have this reminder of her presence. While I work, I will frequently turn to her and ask for help when I'm struggling or say thank you when something unexpected and useful comes to mind. The very Queen of Heaven is indeed that accessible, that present, that aware of me, no different than if my own mother were sitting here with me. Plus, writing can be a lonely occupation. There is a sorrow mixed in with the joy of it, a kind of necessary death. And Mary knows all about that. Propping up this book is just one small, conscious way for me to invite heaven to join me in this process. I pray even now that she will intercede for me, for clarity and holiness of thought.

And when I look at her through this work of art, I am reminded once again that there is a reason that Mary is the subject of so much wonderful art in the world.

One of the things I appreciate most about the study of art is the widely accepted approach that you study the classics first. My friend, Cristia, clarified this for me: you break down line by line, stroke by stroke, what the masters are doing, how they are achieving their desired results *before* launching off on your own artistic voyage. I have yet to meet a painter or sculptor who resents the contributions of Michelangelo. No one seems to resist the authority of a da Vinci or the mastery of Caravaggio. There seems to be less resentment toward the masters, toward "authority" figures in art, than in other areas of life, like the Church. We allow the masters of art to shape us, to teach us, to offer direction in the way we should go in our own art. It's true in painting, it's true in jazz, it's true in literature, philosophy, and the sciences; and it's true in the spiritual life.

Mary is one of our spiritual masters. She went from anonymous and poor to Queen of Heaven and Earth, and we benefit when we study her "technique" for the spiritual life, when we break down her life, line by line, stroke by stroke. She rises above the rest of us as a spiritual genius, not because she went out and mastered a body of knowledge, but because she humbly bowed at the feet of the Master and allowed him to rule her, body and soul, without condition. Joyfully, she consented to the rigorous demands of love, the heaven-shaped blows of her beloved Creator. Right from the beginning—*Be it done unto me according to your word*—she would be his living sculpture.

Adrienne von Speyr reflects on Mary's *fiat* in this way:

When Mary says to the angel, "Let it be to me according to your word," she allows herself to enter into and become one with the word. She wants the word to put forth its power. And the Word is the Son. She is aware of the greatness of the promise, but not for a moment is she disturbed by the fact that *she* is the chosen one. She does not try to be so conscious of the grace of her position as to attract merit; she simply lets the Word take place. She is the only being in whom it takes place, in whom the Word becomes human life in order to dwell among us.

Mary says Yes to love, but she says Yes out of love. And at this moment she does not suspect that this love is the greatest thing she can do. She does not suspect that, for all ages, she will never stop loving; that her life, up to now kept safe in the love of the triune God and her neighbor, will from now on become a vessel pouring forth nothing but love, spreading out in all directions, constantly growing, constantly being taken up into the greatest reality of all.[12]

With all the saints, as we've noted, but even more purely in Mary, she is not self-conscious but God-conscious, and this eradicates any fantasizing or troublesome thoughts for the future. We can examine the rest of the "lines" of her life and find the same trajectory. She is always, perpetually headed toward heaven, headed home.

> This is Mary at the Annunciation: "Yes. Use me, without my knowing the end result. Use me, set me to my heavenly task." This is Mary whose spirit rejoices, "Great things he has done for me!" This is Mary who pondered in her own heart, "And a sword shall pierce your own soul too." This is Mary at the wedding at Cana: "Do whatever he tells you." And this is Mary at the foot of the cross: an exposed and grippingly raw devotion, keeping her eyes on Jesus, even to the end.[13]

And beyond. This is Mary, too, Michelangelo's Mary, the Mary of the *Pietà*.

HOLDING JESUS

I have already discussed the *Pietà* in our chapter on beauty. I reflect on it once again because I do not want to forget or gloss over this moment in the life of Mary: the death of Jesus. The gift that was given, the Word of her womb, is taken away, to where she knows not. Still, she believes the Word: I will build up the temple in three days. Again, she turns to heaven and does not doubt, but asks, how is this possible?

Mary had to have experienced the death of Jesus in a supremely unique way. She was privileged with carrying the incarnation in her body; she was privileged to raise him, even to witness his passion; she was privileged to hold him in death. No one else knew him so well, experienced as much of him as she. No one else carried him in their body. No one else held him as an infant to feed and nurture, heart to heart. No one felt quite the same loss as she, the mother of Jesus. No one grieves for us in quite the same way as our mothers.

If Michelangelo had imagined Christ crucified lying in the arms of Peter or James or John, it would have captured a moment of mourning, but it would not have captured the *Pietà*. The presence of Mary in the death of her son teaches us more about the value and sorrow and power of Christian death than the presence of any other human being. Observing his passion and death, Mary must have pondered these things in a way that only a mother could.

Jesus asked, "Let this cup pass," and it did not, so he drank it to the bottom. But the fact remains that he did not want to die. He did not seek out death. In the Garden of Gethsemane, he did not shed tears of blood because he was looking forward to death. Poet Denise Levertov describes it this way, "The burden of humanness . . . [was] the humiliation of dread, / cold sweat of wanting to let the whole thing go . . . / not the anticipation of death . . . / was Incarnation's heaviest weight, / but this sickened desire to renege, / . . . those depths where purpose / drifted for mortal moments."[14]

Did heaven ever wish to abandon earth? In *this* moment, did the Son of Man wish to shrink back to a safe heaven, homesick for angels and Abba Father? We may wish to assume that the temptations Jesus suffered were left at Gethsemane because it makes the experience easier on us as observers, fallen and responsible, that once the words were issued, "not my will but yours be done," there was nothing left but firm determination. There is no question of Jesus fulfilling the will of the Father, but if anything frightened Jesus, if anything caused him anguish or agony, Good Friday was it.

And Mary was there. One has to wonder what strength was released between mother and son that day, what potent determination arose from that bond on Good Friday when the humanity and divinity of Jesus stood gazing into one another in perfect love to say, *The time has come.* How much did the presence of the mother help to uphold the Son?

Mary was there, immediately there, not only for the *via crucis* but at the hour of his death, when atonement came to full fruition and the expiation of the world's sin would come to lie limp and lifeless in her lap. Then it follows, the most terrifying moment there is, the unbearable pause between "It is finished" and "He is risen!" The *Pietà* reminds us that, with her body and her whole being, Mary *held* her son in life; she *held* him in death; she *beholds* him in heaven. Out of utter love, *she holds him.* This holding does not end; it moves on with her into eternity where it is increased, expanded in every direction, becoming inclusive of the entire human race.

Holding Heaven

Michelangelo's theology of composition is precise. Jesus' face is turned heavenward, almost smiling, while Mary is placed behind him, cloaked by her son, draped by the fresh wounds of the atonement. Her gaze falls on the Savior. Von Speyr notes of Mary's life that "She keeps in the background so that the whole light falls on [Jesus] and the eyes of believers rest on him. And if, occasionally, she has to say some word or show herself, she only does it to direct attention to him."[15] This was true of her whole life and it was certainly true of this moment, the moment of the *Pietà*. Even her grief does not force her into the foreground. She resists the temptation to thrust herself and her broken heart upon the world, to beg that it take notice and grieve *for* her, not *with* her. As Jesus' face is turned heavenward, so Mary's gaze always, unfailingly, falls on Jesus.

If Mary's whole life was glorifying the Lord—her *whole* life— then the *Pietà* tells us what to do in our own moments of *Pietà*: we hold the atonement, hold him before heaven. Just like Mary, we hold Jesus in utter love. This is the way we share in the cup, the way we drink it, right down to the bottom.

This is the Mary of earth, our blessed earth-mamma. What of Mary, Queen of Heaven? We might think of the *Pietà* moment as the hinge on the door to heaven. The atonement makes it possible for the door to swing open; Mary's love and intercession adds an extra generous give to the door so it swings wide, wide. Von Speyr adds that

[Mary's] love is very great; not merely does it transcend the Mother's earthly life and, just as she accompanied her Son's life, accompany the life of Christians, continually creating joy, Christian surprise and deeper dedication; it is so great that it also transcends the death of every person. The Mother was there when the Son died, but she is always present when anyone is dying; she makes no distinction in her love between the Son of Man and his brethren. . . . Her love's everlasting fruitfulness is felt particularly where a dying person is afraid he will no longer encounter love; where, at the end of his life, he realizes that he has loved too little, believed and hoped too little. Then she takes loving steps, encouraging new love, new hope and faith to sprout. The form this takes is, "Let it be to me according to your word," for the dying man can do nothing but let things happen, unquestioningly and in total surrender. [16]

Thus she held Jesus in life; thus did she hold him in death. And isn't this so often the way a mother prays, by holding? With arms more real and solid and immutable than Michelangelo's marble, she holds us too, in utter love, praying, *now and at the hour of our death.*

THE QUEEN COMES HOME

And what of the hour of hers? We remember that Mary at the moment of *fiat* turned herself over to the Master, body and soul. She became his possession in her entirety, and when she died he came to claim her in her entirety, eager to introduce her to her eternal heritage. Mary was assumed into heaven because it was the only fitting reality, the only possible response to her bodily death. The Incarnation could not make himself at home in anything less than the purest dwelling; such a vessel would not, could not be left to rot in a tomb.

Through the grace of God, St. Joseph of Cupertino, our flying friar, broke the laws of gravity with the overruling law of love. So, too, through the love of heaven, Mary was not subject to the laws of natural decay and corruption. Her devotion overruled them, and her body, that place where the Word dwelled in flesh and fluid, blood and bone, was taken up and changed in an instant. She did not ascend into heaven as Jesus did, rising on her own power. Rather, heaven reached down and brought her home. Once again, finally and forever, she surrendered completely to the Master. And once again, in the assumption, as with every major event and quiet, hidden moment of Mary's life, it was the Master who was magnified.

> The Mother was assumed bodily into heaven. But this assumption was so complete and perfect and glorious that it was too much for her alone. . . . She wishes to communicate this grace of the heavenly encounter so that the dying person need not stare solely at death and judgment but can look to the grace granted to the Mother and the mediation of all graces . . . the loss of earth opens up the gaining of heaven.[17]

Mary's assumption also brushes up against one of the greatest mysteries of our own death. It reminds us that God has lasting plans for our bodies, even after we die. St. Paul writes, "Listen, I will tell you a mystery! We will not all die, but we will all be changed, in a moment, in the twinkling of an eye, at the last trumpet. For the trumpet will sound, and the dead will be raised imperishable, and we will be changed" (1 Corinthians 15:51-52).

Death, though we barely begin to know how, is not the final end for our earthly bodies. In the "loss of earth," we "gain heaven," even in our flesh. Though we must wait for the second coming, like Mary, we will be raised and changed in that instant.

Tertullian said that "the flesh is the hinge of salvation." Indeed. Mary's assumption affirms the importance of keeping this notion ever in mind: our earthly bodies are soul-temples designed to glorify God. The Word became flesh and dwelt among us, this flesh of Jesus, this flesh born of Mary, and we share in this great mysterious flesh-and-soul connection.

We remember this, too. Mary's assumption—and even the most devout Catholic misses this sometimes, so let's be clear—does not magnify Mary in glory, it magnifies the glory of God. She would have it no other way. "My soul magnifies the Lord," she exclaims to her cousin Elizabeth. "My spirit rejoices in God my Savior." You see, even then, she was fluent in the language of eternity. She understood perfectly that this is the work of heaven: *glory to the Father*, *glory to the Son*, and *glory to the Holy Spirit*. And for her mastery of this spiritual axiom, she is showered in honor in heaven and venerated throughout earth in every generation.

Holy Mary, Mother of God, pray for us now and at the hour of our death. Amen.

1. *Catechism of the Catholic Church* (Vatican City: Libreria Editrice Vaticana, 1997), 1026.

2. *Catechism*, 1029.

3. Chesterton, *St. Thomas Aquinas and St. Francis of Assisi* (San Francisco: Ignatius Press, 1974), 22.

4. Balthasar, *Light of the Word*, trans. Dennis D. Martin (San Francisco: Ignatius Press, 1993), 352.

5. "Order my love within me," Augustine, *Confessions*, XI.

6. Balthasar, *Light of the Word*, 44.

7. Pope John Paul II, Catechesis on the Holy Angels, *L'Osservatore Romano* (23 July 1986): 3.

8. Vinita Hampton Wright, *A Catalogue of Angels: The Heavenly, the Fallen, and the Holy Ones Among Us* (Brewster, MA: Paraclete Press, 2006), 55.

9. John Henry Newman, "Sermon 29: The Powers of Nature," in *Parochial and Plain Sermons* (San Francisco: Ignatius Press, 1987), 451.

10. Wright, viii–ix.

11. Quoted in *Catechism of the Catholic Church*, 336.

12. Adrienne von Speyr, *Mystery of Death* (San Francisco: Ignatius Press, 1988), 121–122.

13. Liz Kelly, *May Crowning, Mass, and Merton: 50 Reasons I Love Being Catholic* (Chicago: Loyola Press, 2006), 51–52.

14. Denise Levertov, "Salvator Mundi: Via Crucis," *Selected Poems*, ed. Paul A. Lacey (New York: New Directions Books, 2002), 182.

15. Von Speyr, 123.

16. Von Speyr, 123.

17. Von Speyr, 124.

6.

Joy and Sorrow in a City Called Heaven

The home of joy is God. We are God's colonies,
and he visits his colonies.

—Peter Kreeft

I am a poor pilgrim of sorrow
I'm tossed in this wide world alone.
No hope have I for tomorrow.
So, I've started to make heaven my home.

Sometimes I am tossed and driven, Lord.
Sometimes I don't know where to roam.
But I've heard of a city called heaven.
And I started to make it my home.

—A City Called Heaven, a traditional spiritual

My life has been deeply informed by music. Some of my earliest memories converge around not sights but sounds. One in particular springs to mind. It was winter, I think a cold January, and my mother and I were driving through the Twin Cities. I was little and tired. We'd had a big day in the big city, and I was resting my head in her lap as she drove. The heater was blowing on my feet, swallowed up in snow boots dangling over the edge of the front seat. In the corners of the car's windows, an icy, white web of frost threatened to creep in, at war with the defroster.

In the Cities, my mother could tune to a local jazz station. I can still recall looking up from my vantage point there in her lap to catch her delight—really more like relief—when the dial she was turning finally rested with clarity on the deep voice of a woman singing a lazy, low line of improv. She was accompanied by an upright bass and a drummer playing with brushes, pushing with a resonant, slow swish-swish, his left and right hands steadily exchanging circles across the face of the snare. A piano skittered lightly behind her, filling in now and then when she trailed off. My mother drove and tapped her thin fingers cloaked in leather gloves on the steering wheel. She hummed and bobbed her head a bit and seemed entirely at peace, resting with the sounds emanating from the dashboard.

Though young, I knew something of music because all my older siblings played instruments, two of them drums and percussion. In fact my ears still recall with perfect clarity the rudimentary practice sessions that would fill our basement—*flam para-did-dle-diddle, flam para-diddle-diddle*. Still, it would be many years later when I would identify what my ear heard that day as "the blues." Even then, driving through the frozen winter streets of a Midwestern city, resting in the lap of my dear mom who drifted off into the music, my long love affair with jazz had begun.

Later I would learn how much this music grew up out of suffering, how much it had borrowed from spirituals. Those deep, visceral moans that seemed to rise up out of the earth itself, crying for relief, believing in that "land of rest," trusting in a saving Jesus, hoping in heaven, vigorously delighting in the promise of a promised land. I loved jazz so much because it seemed real to me, built on something substantial and weighty, unlike the saccharine, airbrushed pop tunes that the music industry was beginning to grind out like widgets on an assembly line. Jazz had deep roots in real life, real people, real sufferings, and real joys. In an ironic way, it challenged every moment of entitlement and self-pity I ever had. It was not easy music, but it was joyful, and it sharpened me.

I came to believe, too, that the spirituals, which jazz leaned on so heavily for inspiration, possessed a unique kind of wisdom: not just "Christian" lyrics but even more specifically, an eternal perspective. They fastened themselves entirely to the hope of heaven. I sensed and was attracted to the notion that, when invited, heaven still speaks through jazz, still sprinkles heaven all over the *swingin'* earth. When I sing, or when I'm listening to jazz, this is the string that I reach back and pluck, those resonant voices and spirits that longed for "deep river, Lord, I want to cross over into campground."

The spirituals were profoundly oriented toward eternity. One of the greatest achievements of the anonymous, oppressed masses who sang them into existence was that they had no difficulty in conveying heaven as a reality, an actual place one would occupy like your own home. Heaven was not lost as an esoteric idea to those who filled the fields of tobacco plantations with music; to them, heaven was real. And the natural longing that we all have for heaven sat right at the surface of daily life; it was readily accessible, not buried or ignored, not swatted away like an annoying insect. Longing for heaven was nothing to be ashamed of, not a sign of weakness, but a source of inner strength. And a great source of joy.

When we speak of spirituals, we often think of the sorrow that accompanies them, and that's understandable. Like the early Church, whose brutal martyrdoms were not long forgotten but fresh in the minds and spirits of our earliest brethren, the suffering that the slaves endured must have made Christ's cross much less foreign, more available for inspiration. They must have understood it in a profound way, a way that is lost to many of us.

Still, they knew that the story does not end with the cross. They found absolute delight in the contemplation of heaven, not as a cosmic escape hatch, but heaven for heaven's sake, heaven for all the promises it would keep, including holy and eternal Company.

Consider the surprise and delight of the soul who sings, "How I Got Over":

How I got over, How did I make it over?
You know my soul look back and wonder:
How did I make it over?

Soon I will see Jesus,
The Man that died for me,
The One who bled and suffered,
As He hung on Calvary.

I'm gonna view the host in white,
They been tusslin' day and night,
Comin' up from every nation;

They're on their way to the great coronation,
Comin' from the north, south, east, and west,
They on their way to a land of rest.

And then I'm gonna join the heavenly choir,
You know I'm gonna sing and never get tired,
And then I'm gonna sing somewhere roun' God's altar,
And then I'm gonna shout all my trouble over . . .

How did I make it over?

This isn't a suffering soul but a jubilant, grateful, wonderstruck pilgrim come home. If we believe it—that heaven is joining the heavenly choir, singing around God's altar, celebrating "the great coronation"—wouldn't this fill our lives with deep, resonant, and immovable joy?

Some scholars have suggested that the particularly jubilant nature of traditional southern gospel music on Sundays was the equal and opposite reaction to the oppression faced all week. Sunday was an opportunity to throw open wide the door to the human heart and let all the turbulent mixture of agony, suffering, joy, and hope come tumbling out. Then they would gather it all back up in their hearts again, tight and cloistered, for one more week. This must be true. But I wonder if this isn't also true: that there was less of a battle to believe in heaven, to claim it as truth. No one was telling them that heaven was a ridiculous myth. Their innocence may have been robbed in every other area of life, but in their belief they remained as children. When hell circled all about them, tortured them, separated them from their families, stripped them violently of their human dignity, they found heaven, real and ready and waiting every Sunday to restore all that had been lost, and more. The egregious sorrows of slavery were put to rest, sabbath rest—at least for the day. They chose, again and again in their music, to live with eternal perspective.

The spirituals are so invigorating and valuable, not only for what they teach us of surviving great suffering but for what they teach us of heaven's joy. We tend to think of joy and sorrow as polarized opposites, north and south poles of the human experience, but I think this is wrong. Joy is simply sorrow all grown up. Joy is sorrow transfigured; it is suffering transformed. That's why heaven is full to the brim with it despite its full knowledge of the earth's agonies. As Peter Kreeft writes, "Joy is the life of heaven,"[1] because, like the finest wine, everyone there has been spiritually "aged" to absolute perfection, and the joy in that refinement is as golden and beaming and uncontainable as the sun.

AN AWFUL GRACE

Such joy is able to pierce even the darkest, vilest, most hidden pool of human suffering. Yet, it remains a challenge to rectify these things: a joyful heaven hovering over a suffering earth. Who among us has not wondered at a heaven ordered toward joy when things like AIDS, cancer, the Rwandan genocide, abortion, or contemporary slavery rage across the face of the earth? Is heaven indifferent, perpetually partying even as we trudge away in the dark trenches of sin, suffering, and death? *Certainly not*, you say, but can you prove it? How can the two possibly coexist? How can there be so much joy in *that* place when there is so much obvious suffering in *this* place? As Christians, we must gather up language and prayers and means by which we can express an eternal perspective, always and especially in the face of egregious suffering and injustice because they so frequently push people away from heaven and the Church.

Perhaps the problem is that we don't know how to receive trials and suffering. Our trials tempt us to cling to the earth and cast resentful glances toward heaven, as though paradise were owed to us. How desperately many of us need dramatic reorientation, eternal recalibration. St. John of the Cross says that contemplation of the cross is *the* way to joy. We must remember that Jesus, though innocent, experienced the sorrow of earth most fully in his passion and death. He is no stranger to pain and suffering, or that most excruciating betrayal of abandonment by one's friends, and neither will any Christian be; rather, suffering rightly received is one of our most valuable opportunities to grow in holiness. When joined to the cross of Christ it is redemptive, and this is a mystery more to be embraced and lived out than to be explained, although volume after volume has been written on the subject. Whole religious orders have devoted themselves to its contemplation, like the Passionists who take vows to carry Christ's passion and death in their very hearts. They know: sorrow is a wise teacher; suffering is a spiritual genius.

During a particularly protracted and frightening trial in my life, at a point when my hope had simply run out, a dear friend e-mailed me this quote from the Greek poet, Aeschylus: "He who learns must suffer. And even in our sleep, pain that cannot forget falls drop by drop upon the heart, and in our own despair, against our will, comes wisdom to us by the awful grace of God." Is it possible, could it be, that the most painful experience of your life was (or is), in fact, a gift—an awful grace—from heaven?

To address this idea fully would take much more than this chapter, much more than a book, but I ask you to prayerfully consider, in whatever agony you currently suffer, is it possible that you might find heaven somewhere in the mix? Is there a way in which you can invite heaven's joy to enter in through this sorrow, to refine your sorrow into heavenly joy? Is it possible that this great suffering is really a personal invitation issued by the very hand of heaven to enter into eternal joy?

In response to our suffering, it is the most natural prayer in the world: *Dear Lord, save me, end this, remove this pain from my life!* But when sorrow begins to grow up, the prayer becomes, *Your will be done, oh Lord, on earth as it is in heaven. Thank you for this trial, and if I am to suffer still more, please use it, redeem it, do not let it go to waste.* In the Christian life, in a life lived with eternal perspective, the objective will never be to outrun sorrow and suffering. Instead, the life lived from an eternal perspective looks to the end, even if sometimes with great and terrible strain, for heaven's agenda. It reads every experience on earth through the lens of paradise and finds acceptance and contentment in all things. In the end, it finds surprising joy.

I am reminded of one of my favorite Chaim Potok novels, *The Chosen*, about a young, orthodox Jewish boy who has been raised "in silence." From childhood, Danny demonstrated extraordinary intelligence, including nearly perfect recall. His father, a highly respected rabbi in his community, had only one desire for his son: that he would become a *tzaddik*, a holy man. When he began to notice, however, that Danny was beginning to look down on other children who were not as intelligent, he made the terrible and difficult decision to raise the boy "in silence." It was the only way that he knew how to teach the boy compassion for others. He never spoke directly to him again; never played with him affectionately as he did his other children; would only ever converse with him when they were studying Jewish law. Danny had no idea why this was happening, and the pain of this rejection was excruciating. Throughout the novel, one wonders at how much Danny must have missed his father; but in the end, we wonder how much the father must have missed his son as well.

As the novel nears its conclusion, one thing becomes very clear: Danny has indeed become a compassionate man, wise and gentle, with a great desire to use his intelligence to help others. At the climax of the book, when Danny asks permission to study psychology, Danny's father not only gives Danny his blessing, he declares that Danny would be "a *tzaddik* for the world." He was finally able to explain his actions to his son, and the silence was lifted. What Danny had once imagined to be inexplicable cruelty he now saw was the greatest sacrifice of love his father could have given him. In a joyous concluding scene, Danny tells his best friend, "We talk all the time now."

What a fitting description of heaven: we are restored to perfect communion once again with our Father. Heaven will be that place where "we talk all the time," and where we will come to understand that our greatest sufferings were also our greatest gifts.

"Joy," writes Kreeft, "comes not from the world, through the body (like pleasure) or from ourselves, through the soul (like happiness) but from God, through the spirit, it 'smells of divinity.'"[2] Take careful note of his distinctions. Suffering has that same aroma; it has such tremendous potential to become the odor of sanctity because it brings us gifts that simply could not come to us by any other route. The grace and miracle of redemption required the cross, though the cross certainly gave no pleasure to heaven. What it gave, what the cross created, was not pleasure, not happiness, but joy.

Meeting with "Eucatastrophe"

Joy isn't "all smiles." It doesn't grin. It burns from the center of one's being; it aches all the way through to the core of eternity. We must not confuse it with ease or pleasure but recognize that it is, in fact, paradoxically of the same lineage as suffering.

Certainly, no Catholic is a stranger to paradox. A portion of the great genius of the Church is her recognizing the need to hold in perfect, dynamic tension a whole host of paradoxical pairings. In fact the faith is built on what Robert Hugh Benson calls the "Paradox of paradoxes," the incarnation. Jesus was the supreme example of living paradox. He was carpenter and king. He became *human* in order that he might reveal his *divinity*. The psalmist declares, "You are the most handsome of men; / grace is poured upon your lips" (Psalm 45:2), but Isaiah answers, "he had no form or majesty that we should look at him, / nothing in his appearance that we should desire him" (Isaiah 53:2). In the Gospel of John, Jesus declares, "The Father and I are one" and "the Father is greater than I" (John 10:30; 14:28). He proclaims that "those who find their life will lose it, and those who lose their life for my sake will find it" (Matthew 10:39). In the spiritual reality he completes, the meek shall inherit the earth and the lion will lie down with the lamb. Thus, paradox naturally and easily inhabits our faith.

Chesterton writes, "The cross, though it has at its heart a collision and a contradiction, can extend its four arms for ever without altering its shape. Because it has a paradox in its centre it can grow without changing. The circle returns upon itself and is bound. The cross opens its arms to the four winds; it is a signpost for free travelers."[3] The joy of heaven joins in this mystery as it reconciles itself with the sorrows of daily life.

J. R. R. Tolkien, imaginative genius that he was, might help us to digest part of this paradox more thoroughly: that from an eternal perspective, suffering is joy, or at least has that tremendous potential. Who better to discuss the greatest "happy ending" ever told than the man who mastered the "happy ending" in his fantastic tales like *Lord of the Rings*? While heaven is no fairy tale, Tolkien's highly lauded essay, "On Fairy Stories," explores how the "happy ending" of such stories speak to the ultimate, eternal happy ending that Christians hope for in heaven. As he writes in reference to the gospel story, "There is no tale ever told that men would rather find was true."[4]

Tolkien, who invented whole and thoroughly convincing imaginary languages for his characters, uses a wonderful invented word in the essay: *eucatastrophe*. (When I first read the essay, incidentally, I misread the word as "eucharist-trophe," which was wrong, but as it turns out, a useful and rather telling error.) Tolkien defines *eucatastrophe* in the fairy story as a redemption, a turning point where an impossible but entirely believable grace enters the tale to rescue and redeem the faithful. And, just like the "happy ending" of heaven, a *eucatastrophe*, is not a tidy "eject" button but a "good catastrophe." He writes,

> The consolation of fairy-stories, the joy of the happy ending: or more correctly, of the good catastrophe, the sudden joyous turn (for there is no true end to any fairy-tale): this joy, which is one of the things which fairy-stories can produce supremely well, is not essentially "escapist" or "fugitive." In its fairy-tale—or otherworld—setting, it is a sudden and miraculous grace; . . . it does not deny the existence of . . . sorrow and failure: the possibility of these is necessary to the joy of deliverance; it denies (in the face of much evidence, if you will) universal final defeat . . . giving a fleeting glimpse of Joy, Joy beyond the walls of the world, poignant as grief.[5]

This is another useful definition for heaven: "Joy beyond the walls of the world."

Like Tolkien's *eucatastrophe*, heaven does not deny the very real sorrow of life; rather, in the face of monumental evidence to the contrary, it destroys the universal, final defeat we know as death. To accomplish this, it enlists sorrow, transforms it to become a vehicle for "the joy of deliverance." We remember how beauty points to something beyond itself. So too sorrow, sorrow rightly received and transfigured by God's grace, always points to joy. It is this joy, heaven's joy, we taste in the Eucharist, that sudden and miraculous grace made possible by a grueling passion and death, and later an empty tomb. It is this joy we taste in all the sacraments, especially the moment of absolution for the contrite. We taste it in beauty and the company and communion of holy people. This is the joy we taste when we make of our lives, like Mary, like the saints, a total gift of self, despite how much that costs us. This joy is "otherworldly."

Tolkien writes, "It is the mark of a good fairy-story . . . that . . . to child or man that hears it, when the 'turn' comes, [there is] a catch of the breath, a beat and lifting of the heart, near to (or indeed accompanied by) tears."[6] Doesn't this sound familiar? Haven't we all experienced something profoundly similar in the moment of revelation and redemption? And isn't revelation all the sweeter, all the more joyful, for our having tasted the bitterness of sorrow?

Imagine Mary on Easter morning. Just as the darkness of night begins to lift, she is finding her way in the dark to the tomb, carrying her heavy grief like a sobbing child clutching her chest. Mary Magdalene is at her side, the Blessed Mother surely helping to carry her grief, too. The sorrow is so sharp it is like a dagger through the heart, a blade with no handle; to touch it is to be cut. And even heavier than the grief is the burden of belief, despite so much evidence to the contrary, that Christ will "raise the temple in three days."

But then, the turn comes, "a catch of breath"; she meets with *eucatastrophe*: a stone rolled away and angels appearing to say, "He is risen." With a "lifting of the heart," the question rushes to the surface, *Can it be true?*

Tolkien writes that "the peculiar quality of the 'joy' in successful Fantasy [is] a sudden glimpse of the underlying reality or truth. It is not only a 'consolation' for the sorrow of this world, but a satisfaction, and an answer to that question, 'Is it true?'"[7] Sorrow begs the same question of joy. Sorrow that is growing up leans forward across eternity's banquet table, leads with the heart, and tilts an eager and hopeful ear, asking, *Is heaven true?*

How do you imagine joy responds? If angels came to visit (and we know they do), what do you imagine they would sing in reply?

A God at Play

With all our necessary work and marveling at how God can transform sorrow into joy, we mustn't imagine that God does not delight, just to delight. The joys of heaven are so real and robust and powerful, they continually break forth upon the earth. In fact, creation must have been accompanied by holy delight, even hilarity. As the Father's children, we are given an inheritance in this great, pure joy.

The moon is wonderful evidence for this. It seems to me that she is a rather mirthful planet, like a small child who's been granted permission to stay up way past her bedtime, or maybe she is simply delighted with her assignment: the world's nightlight.

I am particularly fond of flying at night for the view it provides of the moon. She seemed especially bright and steady on a recent flight across the ocean, en route to Rome. She shone down on the wing, hovering high above the clouds, reminiscent of a holy host in adoration, the clouds stretched out beneath her, reaching for the horizon. For a time, she hovered directly outside my window, keeping me company, and there was nothing in between us, just clear, silent, crisp space. As the rest of the plane slept, crouched and crumpled in seats not meant for sleeping bodies, we gazed at one another and giggled like school chums at staying up late. I knew her secrets, and she knew mine. And there was joy.

But then our plane, chasing east, began to separate us. She smiled through the window, lingering over my shoulder a long while, leaving only gradually, until she finally disappeared as my plane drifted ever into dawn.

All I could think of, watching the sun rise outside my window, bidding my moon-girl good night, is that this God of heaven I adore, sometimes, surely, is a God at play.

Chesterton writes, "Man is more himself, man is more manlike, when joy is the fundamental thing in him, and grief the superficial. Melancholy should be an innocent interlude, a tender and fugitive frame of mind; praise should be the permanent pulsation of the soul. Pessimism is at best an emotional half-holiday; joy is the uproarious labour by which all things live."[8]

This is part of why beauty is so transcendent. It's why we paint paintings and coo over babies, saying, "Welcome to the world, little one." It's why mountain hikes in Alaska and the mesas of New Mexico at sunset lift our spirits and fill our eyes with peace. It's why enjoying a really fine meal on the Piazza Navona in Rome while the Bernini fountains bubble in the background nearly guarantees a good night's sleep. It's why coming home to find your roommate playing her violin with the windows thrown open wide, a Roman sun pouring in and a Bach sonata flowing out, helps us to hear the laughter of angels and saints, and yes, even Jesus.

There is joy to be had in this world, unadulterated, pure, heavenly joy. You were created for it. You are most yourself when you are deeply in touch with it. Joy is heaven's prose style; it carries heaven's narrative forward. It is heaven's air and water, its blood and bone and sinew. Joy is heaven's great, eternal story.

Joy turns to the last page of every book of life, it turns to the happy ending, the *eucatastrophe*, and captures a piercing glimpse of heaven. It turns the pencil on end again, and there, from an eternal perspective, breath catches, spirits lift, a gleam comes through. Sorrow has its answer.

1. Peter Kreeft, *Heaven: The Heart's Deepest Longing* (San Francisco: Ignatius Press, 1989), 135.

2. Kreeft, 133. For a deeper examination of the differences between happiness, pleasure, and joy, read Kreeft's section entitled, "A Map of Joy," 124–133.

3. G. K. Chesterton, *St. Thomas Aquinas and St. Francis of Assisi* (San Francisco: Ignatius Press, 1974), 24.

4. J. R. R. Tolkien, *The Tolkien Reader* (New York: Random House, 1966), 89.

5. Tolkien, 85–86.

6. Tolkien, 86.

7. Tolkien, 88.

8. Chesterton, 169.

7.

A Few Final Things

"Those who drink of the water that I will give them will never be thirsty. The water that I will give will become in them a spring of water gushing up to eternal life."
—John 4:14

"Very truly, I tell you, anyone who hears my word and believes him who sent me has eternal life, and does not come under judgment, but has passed from death to life."
—John 5:24

Memento mori—Keep your death in mind.

They are more commonly referred to as "the last things": death, judgment, heaven, and hell. Since this whole book is a reflection on heaven, I will take the liberty of altering the combination and focus on death, judgment, purgatory, and hell.

My brother, a seminarian, recently gave a talk on the last things to a group of high school students. He noted that, although we tend to complicate these pieces of our faith life, they're really quite simple. As an introduction, he briefly summarized them, saying, "Death and judgment are two actions; we die and are judged. Heaven and hell are two destinations. Heaven is good; hell is bad; . . . and purgatory is just a step on the way to heaven. Everyone in purgatory gets to heaven." Though he was tempted to end the lesson there, much to the delight of his young charges, he examined them more fully. And so will I.

The last things are simple. Still, these are big words, heavy words thick with meaning. When they show up at your door, they are not alone; rather, they often bring a lot of emotional, social, and cultural baggage. These words, as much as any, like to hang us up, keep us out of the confessional, keep us at arm's length with heaven. Sometimes, they like to chase away eternal perspective and turn up the volume on fear or resentment. When they are misshapen, abused, misunderstood, they like to keep Jesus at bay.

As we move through these next chapters, I'd ask you to think about these things in terms of the attributes and virtues of heaven and our heavenly Father, which they embody. Dante had his Beatrice; imagine that when you die, as you face death and judgment, if you so choose, these will be your guides: justice and mercy. May we heed them even now on earth, for they know precisely the way to that eternal place where their Master dwells. They know the way home to Love.

Death: A Holy Harvest

By mid-September in Minnesota, the evenings take on the first signs of winter's approaching chill, and the temperatures begin to dip down and down. After dinner, we sit in a semicircle around the wood stove in the old log cabin part of the house, our feet stretched toward it, catching the heat for the rest of our bodies, and there we make our plans—to chop more wood, to butcher the ducks, to cover the strawberry beds.

Outside, nature and all of the creatures of her dominion simply know to prepare. Take our horse, Shadow, for instance. His summer coat, so sleek and shining like fresh black licorice, begins to take on the gentle fuzzy down of a new duckling. Each morning he's grown just a bit more furry, a touch more round with warm winter horse-plume. Or, the once lush green fields around us that were so rich with vegetation, at one time so hungry for full bloom, now begin to give way to autumn reaping. Fading golden stalks of corn stand like platoons of old soldiers, grown weary with standing at attention. They rustle through their ranks when fall breezes blow with the dry stiffness that announces harvest.

Harvest is coming. Endings approach.

I am curiously, occasionally envious of creatures and living things which know their place without question, who respond to their natural circumstances innately. Shadow needs no one to whisper reminders in his ear, no sticky notes from me in his stall to say, "Fatten up! Winter is coming!" The pony simply knows to prepare.

Or, imagine how restful it is be to be a stalk of corn that knows only to grow and grow, all of its life spent reaching up to the sun, all of its energy fixed on its end, fixed on harvest and a job well done. No wondering about what else it might be—a bean or a rosebush—no wishing it might live a little while longer, or how it might prefer to spend its summer in the Berkshires or on the coast of Maine. It simply grows and grows, until harvest comes.

Mortal things need no reminders of their mortality; they move toward a natural end without distraction or denial. But immortal creatures, like you and me, we need to be reminded that we "also must be ready, for the Son of Man is coming at an unexpected hour" (Matthew 24:44). We need coaching to prepare for death and all that lies beyond. We need instruction to understand that this life on earth is already infused with heaven, that this life and the next are intimately, eternally related. They are made body-and-blood relatives through the passion, death, and resurrection of Christ.

Jesus' mercy is never greater than when he exhorts us to prepare for his Father's house, to cultivate an eternal perspective. Just as he encouraged us not to be afraid of earthly trappings, he reminded us to "store up for yourselves treasures in heaven" (Matthew 6:20). We share in this act of mercy when, in love, grace, and holiness, we remind one another to prepare. We share in kingdom work when we sometimes whisper, sometimes roar, "Harvest is coming!"

IN WITH THE CHICKENS

It is good to turn our minds toward the end of life, toward eternal things, for a variety of reasons, not least of which is that Jesus plainly encouraged us to do so. Death is coming. You are closer to it today than yesterday. And in the morning, should you awaken to this world, you will be closer still to death. What will yours be? Will your death be a holy harvest? Does even asking the question make you uneasy? Does death frighten you a little? When the world you know grows dark and finished, and you take your final breath, what do you imagine will happen next?

To contemplate our death is not a call to become overly

engrossed in the morbid. Death is a natural, inevitable part of life—Adam and Eve saw to that. But what makes our deaths so much more interesting than that of the cornstalk is that physical death becomes an entryway to other things, final things, final places, eternal places. Even as it is perfectly natural, it is also perfectly supernatural. It is important that we hold up both lenses simultaneously to the light to capture the full, eternal prism.

In preparing this book, I read a number of mystical accounts of people who experienced heaven, hell, or purgatory in one supernatural way or another. One interview stands out in my mind. It was given by a simple, faithful woman named Maria Simma who lived in the mountains of Austria. Since childhood, she'd prayed fervently for souls in purgatory. Beginning at age twenty-five, she experienced a very unique charism in that she was visited by souls from purgatory. She spoke with them and asked them questions. They frequently asked her to have Masses said on their behalf, and they shared their experience in purgatory with her as an exhortation to the living.

Now, her account of this experience was certainly very interesting and unusual, but her mystical visions did not reveal new or previously hidden information; they only mirrored Church teaching—and this fact adds to their credibility. What captured my attention far more was this: at one point, she interrupted the nun who was interviewing her to say she needed to take a little break to go feed her chickens. She went out, fed her chickens, and returned five minutes later to resume the interview. Just like that. One minute she was describing the soul of a priest in purgatory who had come to visit her to exhort others to accept their sufferings as purgative, and the next minute she was tossing seed to hens.

This unassuming woman who'd been given this incredible gift occupied her humble, holy life without mystical pretenses; she vividly animated the intersection of heaven and earth, the perfect impression and infiltration of the divine order upon and throughout natural order. Her mystical visions were *super*, yes, but they were also *natural*. Her natural, mortal life was so deeply informed by the spiritual and eternal that it was no great feat for her to place the two side by side, day in and day out. For Maria, eternity is in visitations and visions, and it's in the chicken coop.

Likewise, we needn't—and perhaps shouldn't—separate this life and the next, assuming they are spiritual oil and water. Jesus didn't, and neither did Mary nor the saints. Death was not something "other" for them, but simply part of a larger, unified whole. Adrienne von Speyr writes,

> For the Christian life is not merely the implementation of teaching delivered by the Son, adapted and limited to the needs of time and space; it stretches out to the mystery of eternity. The believer always has the right to see all his actions under the light of eternity and to expect it to be thus clarified. He no longer needs to take his limitations and his transitory nature as immutably given; here and now he can live—in advance, so to speak—on the basis of eternal things . . . in stamping his transitory, temporal existence with the mark of eternal duration he will not be doing anything inappropriate or unlawful, for both Son and Mother have entrusted him

with the mystery of their death and resurrection, which are so intertwined that the unity they manifest applies to him too.

The believer may not approach the tasks of his life here below solely with earthly considerations and perspectives; nor may he put earthly limits on his Christian hope and love—even in matters that seem to be purely human. For he is a citizen of heaven, and his citizenship is one of love. This love, lived out by the Son and his Mother, became so fruitful that the lives of all of us are marked by this mystery.[1]

Von Speyr recommends life and death as unified gifts given by heaven precisely "so that we may experience something of what Mother and Son have experienced on earth and in heaven." We are not to be struck merely by isolated details of their lives; rather, we are to grasp their whole inseparably earthly and eternal being as the revelation of a single, triune mystery. Life and death are universal and unified experiences. We are all earthly and eternal beings.

We recall our image of the pencil turned on end: death, like all of life, is incorporated in the point; death is infused with eternity—that same eternity that visits us in visions and in the chicken coop.

FORGETTING FINALS

Perhaps when one is young and in good health, it requires more pointed effort to contemplate death and judgment. I am no longer a young person; neither am I old, but what a growing Christian faith is teaching me is that, while my earthly life is a tremendously important and valuable gift, this earthly life will not be the best or most interesting experience I will ever have. Do you believe that?

Imagine a new heaven and a new earth, and the potential for a new you eternally in it: doesn't this sound mighty appealing? Isn't this why Paul says, "to die with Christ is gain?" When he says, "Set your minds on things that are above, not on things that are on earth, for you have died, and your life is hidden with Christ in God" (Colossians 3:2-3). Paul is assuring us that "things above" are better, *infinitely* better for us to contemplate. I think of my dear St. Joseph of Cupertino, thrilled to finally fall deathly ill, and I wonder, am I that convinced of eternal blessedness? Am I that in love with the reality of perfect communion with the Beloved?

And if not, why not? As Christians, why in the world would we send death indefinitely to the "timeout" corner of our daily experience like a naughty child, only to be summoned for contemplation at some much, much, *much* later date? Why do we forget final things?

Maybe, in part, because we don't enjoy reflecting on the consequences. Regis Martin writes that

> eschatological forgetfulness, especially on the part of Christians, will simply force the world to look elsewhere for information and consolation about the End. When men cease to hear the truth about Death or eternal life from Christians, the truth that it is their chief business to dispense, they will not blunder forth like nihilists believing nothing. No, they will more than likely hear and believe anything.[2]

Relativism has sneaked its way into sacred places, taking root in soil meant to grow eternal things. Again, we need reminders to prepare. We need to hear again and again that the unique and glorious suffering of Christ's cross re-situates and reorders the world. It revalues death. As Balthasar observes, "Instead of fearing death as the final evil and begging God for a few more years of life, as the weeping king Hezekiah does, Paul would like most of all to die immediately in order 'to be with the Lord' (Philippians 1:23)."[3]

Naturally then, Balthasar says, along with death, the cross revalues life: "If we live, we live to the Lord; if we die, we die to the Lord (Romans 14:8)." Furthermore, the cross alters our very "existence before God and our being judged by him. All of us were sinners before him and worthy of condemnation. But God 'made the One who knew no sin to be sin, so that we might be justified through him in God's eyes' (2 Corinthians 5:21)."[4] And this is the truth we are charged with dispensing. Does your life bear this out?

Long before he became pope, the Holy Father, Pope Benedict XVI, wrote in an Easter meditation, "Holy Saturday: the day God was buried; isn't this remarkably true of our day, today? Is not our century starting to be one long Holy Saturday, the day God was absent?"[5] Words like "judgment" send our century's skin to crawling because they uproot a comfortable relativism that has convinced us that earth is as good as it gets. If you have come to such a conclusion, one episode of evening news might cloak you in utter despair.

The Messiah is not missing; it is only that our devastating illiteracy in the language of eternity has darkened our ability to perceive him. A thousand mindless distractions are keeping us from our studies in eternity. You and I know God is not absent; his holy heaven is everywhere. It is our Christian privilege to remind the world that heaven isn't empty by speaking its language fluently in our lives. Nietzsche was dead wrong; God is not dead.

Which means, neither is sin.

The Fact of Sin and the Grace of Judgment

One day, as I was passing by the television, what I heard on the evening news made my stomach wrench. A public official had been arrested for making arrangements to have sex with a five-year-old girl. As part of a sting operation over the Internet, an agent posing as the child's mother offered the child "for hire," and the perpetrator responded with as much casual attention as he might bring to buying a used toaster.

The child was *five*.

How long, oh Lord, will you endure us?

Even the hardest heart on earth must admit, must concede, how wrong this is. Even the most nonreligious in the bunch must be tempted to utter, "*That* is a sin."

Yet, in the face of such unspeakable evil, there is tremendous consolation that we can identify it as such. It teaches us that sin is knowable, identifiable; it carries a definition and consequences.

In our current culture, even the most modest notion of sin has become almost passé. G. K. Chesterton said it marvelously in *Orthodoxy*:

Modern masters of science are much impressed with the need of beginning all inquiry with a fact. The ancient masters of religion were quite equally impressed with that necessity. They began with the fact of sin—a fact as practical as potatoes. Whether or not man could be washed in miraculous waters, there was no doubt at any rate that he wanted washing. But certain religious leaders . . . have begun in our day not to deny the highly disputable water, but to deny the indisputable dirt. . . .

In this remarkable situation it is plainly not now possible (with any hope of a universal appeal) to start, as our fathers did, with the fact of sin. This very fact which was to them (and is to me) as plain as a pikestaff, is the very fact that has been specially diluted or denied.[6]

Maybe our neighbors and friends find our doctrines on judgment a little too "fire and brimstone" for their taste (or our talk of heaven too saccharine). When we eradicate sin as a reality, however, we also eradicate the love that makes heaven possible. St. Augustine writes in *City of God* that "eternal life is the Supreme Good, and eternal death the Supreme Evil, and that to achieve the one and avoid the other, we must live rightly." And this of course assumes that there is a right way to live—and, therefore, logically, a wrong way.

As Chesterton points out, believing in the fact of sin wasn't always so far out of fashion. Michelangelo, for example, sinner and genius that he was, certainly had no problem imagining judgment, the great justice of God. His sweeping magnum opus, the *Last Judgment*, is perhaps one of the most universally recognized works of art in the world. Poised midway up the altar wall of the Sistine Chapel, a youthful and commanding Christ Pantokrator, his arm of judgment raised in perfect authority, towers high above the damned who descend into the horrors of hell in a twist of torsos and terror. Michelangelo had no trouble envisioning a mankind in need of saving from a serious, eternal, burning hell. So where did sin, "plain as a pikestaff," go?

The wry and wonderful Flannery O'Connor, reflecting on the South, tracks the trajectory of sin's disappearance beautifully. She writes,

> The notion of perfectibility of man came about at the time of the Enlightenment in the 18th century. This is what the South has traditionally opposed. "How far we have fallen" means the fall of Adam, the fall from innocence, from sanctifying grace. The South in other words still believes that man has fallen and that he is only perfectible by God's grace, not by his own unaided efforts. The Liberal approach is that man has never fallen, never incurred guilt, and is ultimately perfectible by his own efforts. Therefore, evil in this light is a problem of better housing, sanitation, health, etc., and all mysteries will eventually be cleared up. Judgment is out of place because man is not responsible.[7]

Not responsible? *Someone* is responsible. And, "enlightened" or not, we know it. We turn on the evening news and see the devastation our sin has wrought and something eternal rises up within us, scalding and sharp to the touch, a holy blade, ready and longing to carve out some real justice upon the world. It is the great secret too many Christians hide; it is the knife we have let go dull: more often than not, we know sin when we see it, the ability issued by an eternal hand.

Justice and judgment are real, and necessary, and they are born from eternity. They are not our creations. They are not *of* this world; they are *in* it. Thank God.

When the world bellows, "It wasn't me!" we know just exactly how far it has fallen.

Do not give in to the tidy temptation that says you do not need saving, that real evil is only reserved for Internet pornographers and those who proliferate genocide, that the atonement is only one of many entrées to be chosen from on some great cosmic menu, that Jesus was just another social activist and not the Savior of the world. Sin is a cunning and tenacious killer of souls. Sin is real, and it's bad. It's in you, and it's in me. No earthly remedy will remove it, no amount of earthly enlightenment will repair its damage; it requires an eternal antidote. The good news is, there is One.

This is where "last things" get really simple again. We either believe him or we don't. "I and my father are one," he says. "No one can come to the Father but through me." Here the two last destinations rise like flags on flagpoles to flap in eternal winds: heaven or hell. We keep always before our eyes the flagship colors of one or the other destination. Will we, who are so inundated with options and choices and variety, be surprised to discover that in "last things" there are only two destinations from which to choose?

Martin reminds us of Augustine's great line, which clarifies the demarcation: "Do not presume; one of the thieves was lost. Do not despair; one of the thieves was saved." And the one who was saved was saved because he recognized justice hanging beside him.

Jesus says, "All authority in heaven and on earth has been given to me" (Matthew 28:18).

And because of his life's masterwork, we believe him. The poetry of Denise Levertov captures it poignantly:

Six hours outstretched in the sun, yes,
hot wood, the nails, blood trickling
into the eyes . . .

Unique
in agony, Infinite strength, Incarnate,
empowered Him to endure
inside of history,
through those hours when He took to Himself
the sum total of anguish and drank
even the lees of that cup.[8]

And this is precisely how long and how much he will endure, how far his arms will stretch out *in* love *for* love of his own.

CHRISTUS REX

When we make "judgment" a dirty word, what we miss is that judgment and love go hand in hand for Jesus. In the eternal equation written by the Father and lived out by the Son, judgment plus love equals justice. Not so much for us. We get justice and revenge all mixed up all the time. Maybe that's why we find it so difficult to believe that our eternal judgment—to be confronted with the truth of ourselves and the truth of eternity—could be a loving, saving kind of gift.

"If we are to discover the character of any people," wrote St. Augustine, "we have only to examine what it loves."[9] Isn't that true? What we love speaks volumes about us. What we love, for better or worse, often dictates how we live, how we spend our time, the direction we go, the choices we make, the kind of creatures we are becoming. It is useful to ask yourself, What do I love? What do my loves reveal about me? (Take those two questions with you for the next few months in prayer and reflect on what God tells you.)

What do you think a "love examination" would say about our culture? As I look around, I see no lack of love. People are wildly in love with many things—youth, power, money, sex, fame, adrenaline. Heaven doesn't seem to rank high among our affections. God doesn't often even make the list. So when it comes to this line in the creed we profess—*He sits at the right hand of the Father and from thence, he shall come to judge the living and the dead*—it would be no wonder if your heart stopped if you believed your judge to be a devourer filled with a deep, fixed, and unflinching hatred for you. Who could love a master like that? But this is to mistake *Christus Rex* for *the accuser*. We suffer from "mercy confusion," just like we suffer from "beauty confusion." In our love affair with political correctness, tolerance, and inclusiveness, we've thrown the judgment-baby out with the bath water. We think we are performing a work of mercy, but all we end up with is a very empty tub.

We tremble and quake at the thought of judgment, and it is right that we should do so, for who among us can cast the first stone? To strip away what Pope Benedict XVI calls "the illusion of my innocence,"[10] and face the final accounting of our lives, answering to God alone without maneuver or self-justification or even support from those on our side—we've got reason to tremble. Regis Martin describes the moment of our death magnificently when he writes, "Each of us will step out from behind the wings of this world, and there, on the other side, across the threshold of death, be ushered into fiery collision with Ultimate Reality itself, the very Pantokrator in whose blazing presence everlasting Judgment falls on every man who has ever lived."[11] How terrifying—and at the same time, *awesome*.

But that is our human response to this divine encounter. The divine experience is one completely flooded with hope and love. Martin continues, writing, "God is the *hoper* who comes in hope for us men, hoping we might bestir ourselves a wee bit on behalf of our own salvation." Then he reminds us of Péguy's great line, "You must have confidence in God. . . . He certainly has had / confidence in us. / He had enough confidence in us to give us, to entrust us with his only Son. / (Alas what we did with Him.)"[12] Pope Benedict says it this way: "Hope in a Christian sense is always hope for others as well. It is an active hope, in which we struggle to prevent things moving towards the 'perverse end'."[13] God's hope for his children is *active*; it seeks our *protection*.

What's more, hope for one's child is not easily quashed. Don't all loving parents naturally hope and hope and hope in their children, no matter what? Does any loving parent *want* to find error that needs correction in their children? Doesn't correction take far more energy, devotion, and commitment than laxity? Does any parent *enjoy* punishing their child?

Jesus appears at our death as judge, yes, and in this he will not diminish himself one bit. He is our eternal judge, but he is also just and gentle. He loves us too much to be lax, to be careless with his creation. And if we think it through, we know, it is precisely his mighty and glorious justice that is so entirely convincing, which compels our hearts to love and adore him, even when, *especially* when, we come out of our hiding and stand beneath the gaze of the One who reveals all.

Justice—that is, judgment plus love—is the greatest, most merciful thing there is because it eternally cloaks us in and protects us with truth. God's kingdom is ordered, not only to glory and beauty and joy and homecomings and friendship, but also to the mercy of justice. Heaven isn't heaven without it. Neither is earth—and perhaps that's why we are in such excruciating pain.

Scott Hahn writes, "God's justice, like His mercy, appears everywhere in the Bible. It is an integral part of His self-revelation. To deny the force of divine judgment, then, is to make God less than God, and to make us less than His children. For every father must discipline His children, and paternal discipline is itself a mercy, a fatherly expression of love."[14]

Indeed. Have you ever met a child who is never disciplined by his or her parents? How enjoyable is an undisciplined child? To what kind of life is that child predisposed? Not only will a child raised without discipline grow up likely to hurt himself, he's going to hurt others, too. As Hahn makes plain,

> If God's covenant makes us His family, then sin means more than a broken law. It means broken lives and a broken home. Sin comes from our refusal to keep the covenant, our refusal to love God as much as He loves us. Through sin, we abandon our status as children of God. Sin kills the divine life in us. Judgment, then, is not an impersonal, legalistic process. It is a matter of love, and it is something we choose for ourselves. Nor is punishment a vindictive act. God's "curses" are not expressions of hatred, but of fatherly love and discipline. Like medicinal ointment, they hurt in order to heal. They impose suffering that is remedial, restorative, and redemptive. God's wrath is an expression of His love for His wayward children.[15]

Think of this next time you must punish your children—*you are orienting them toward heaven.* You are lovingly imposing an eternal perspective. You are helping them to rightly order their lives. You are helping them to practice for heaven, because justice—again, judgment plus love—is spoken fluently there.

Remember this, too: the battle for the souls of your children, the battle to raise them up with eternal perspective—this is a war God wants you to win. He's on your side, and he knows every battlefield, every piece of weaponry, and all the sneaking strategies of the enemy and the enemy's army. You will not be abandoned in this quest. You have more influence, and more heavenly help, than you even know.

Purgatory: Aching for Completion

An art history professor of mine once said that when someone questioned Michelangelo on how he achieved *David*, one of his most famous sculptures, he replied, "I simply removed everything that was not David." The spiritual disciplines are designed to work very much like this. In our practice of prayer, fasting, reconciliation, meditation, mortification, and so on, God chips away every thing that is not the real us, the work of art that we are meant to be. He removes all of the extra sin-stone so that our full beauty may be revealed.

Purgatory is simply a continuation of this process post-mortem. Even if we die in God's friendship, we may not yet be perfect; our deepest truest selves, as God intended us to be, may not yet be fully revealed. Purgatory is a great grace in that it allows for any remaining stone of sin to be removed; it frees us to become a part of heaven's masterwork.

During a particularly intense period of prayer while on retreat a few years ago, I had a vivid impression of heaven as a kind of collection of artistic masterpieces—each work of art represented the life of one of God's children, and there we all milled about enjoying one another's lives in paintings and sculptures, mosaics and tapestries. And though these pieces hung on walls and stood on pedestals, they were not dead things, final things, but living and eternal. Each irradiated worship of the Artist, our Maker.

Jesus himself was giving me a tour of his *paradiso* when we turned a corner and suddenly I recognized that we were standing in front of the mosaic of my mother's life. Beauty and clarity and perfect understanding came together in an instant. So many little fractured pieces of glass, so many fragments perfectly, meticulously placed by the loving hands of the Creator. Not one out of place. Not one even slightly askew. Every portion perfectly appointed. Her mosaic glowed and changed constantly with varying reflections of light from various celestial bodies. I saw my mother as heaven saw her, and in that moment she was there standing with me, looking on, running her fingers over the glassy finish and saying, "Didn't he do a good job?"

Then my mother took my arm and said, "Come with me, I want you to see something." We walked further down a hallway and stopped to stand in front of a huge, sweeping, dark canvas. It covered an entire wall; its presence was enormous and brooding and beautiful, like a Caravaggio, playing with the presence of an immutable, penetrating light in the midst of great, oppressive darkness. It was the painting of the life of someone who tormented my mother, and it throbbed with sorrow and despair and bitterness; yet it remained perfectly beautiful. We stood speechless in the presence of the Creator who wrought this work and was completing it. This person, I realized then, did not join us, was not present to observe the work as Jesus and my mother and I had been.

The Father appeared behind us, and I inquired about this person who tormented my mother. He explained, saying, "She will join us one day, but she is not yet a masterpiece. She fought hard against my hand." His voice was soft but full of authority, and great, immeasurable, immoveable love, and somewhere, everywhere, all around us, the prayers of saints and angels rose, humming and holy and resonant, on behalf of this one, who never doubted that God was a lover but was too angry and filled with resentment to receive him. Immediately, I knew my mother and I had already joined in, and it was effortless, perfect joy to pray for this woman.

"Even supposing a man of unholy life were suffered to enter heaven," writes Cardinal Newman, "*he would not be happy there*; so that it would be no mercy to permit him to enter. . . . Heaven is *not* heaven, is not a place of happiness *except* to the holy."[16] Purgatory is a great mercy, an immeasurable and loving gift because it assures our holiness, the key to our eternal happiness. Purgatory remembers that heaven is full of perfectly finished masterpieces, not practice sketches that have been crumpled up and tossed in the trash.

Dressed for Heaven

You might be asking, well, if purgatory is so great and if every soul there is on their way to paradise, why do we refer to them as "the poor souls in purgatory"? It's a valid question.

Imagine that your beloved shows up unannounced, dressed to kill (no pun intended), and wants to whisk you away to a Viennese ball complete with orchestra and feasting—something you've been dreaming of your whole life. But you didn't know that the invitation was coming, that your beloved would simply show up issuing invitations. You are caught off guard, unprepared; you have no idea where you stored your passport; and you just happen to be filthy, in need of a shower and change of clothes. You wouldn't be able to fully enjoy the ball dressed in your dungarees and in need of a good scrub. You would want to prepare yourself.

The great suffering of purgatory—and it must be unimaginable suffering—is knowing that heaven is there, just out of reach, and you are not ready to enter in. It's as though you can hear the music and dancing in the room next door, but cannot yet join the celebration. This is why the saints and mystics, and those souls from purgatory who visited Maria Simma, encouraged us to do our purgatory now, to prepare for heaven now, so that there would be no delay to our arrival in heaven. The pains of anticipation of heaven from a seat in purgatory must be absolutely excruciating. That's why we call them the poor souls; they hear the music and dancing of heaven next door and ache to enter in. They suffer, finally and perfectly, aching for complete, eternal communion with the Beloved.

THE UPRIGHT ON EARTH

There are those who bypass purgatory altogether. We believe Mary did and likely many of the saints. They lived so well on earth, so full of love and eternal beauties, that they had become fluent in heaven's language long before arriving there. But for the rest of us, we ache for holiness, for interpreters of eternity. We long to find it in one another.

Look around. The world is starving to find citizens with integrity: men who keep their promises; women who live in truth, goodness, and beauty; children who honor and respect the ones appointed to provide for them. We long for fellows who keep their word, who will not abandon us in our darkest hour but will stand through to the end at the foot of our crosses, to witness and behold and pray. Our searching eyes scan the horizon, looking to the world's power brokers—in Hollywood, or in the capitals of nations, or in the wealthy kingdoms of Wall Street—only to have our hopes dashed again and again. But a just man, a righteous woman, a grateful child, someone headed for heaven, is often very quiet and humble; such a person draws no attention to themselves. To find someone like this, we have to know where and how to look, to look with interior eyes. People like this have found a way to live such that the stigmata is imprinted on their hearts.

One of the greatest treasures of my life is that I know several men and women just like this, and one gentleman in particular. He is genuinely delighted at the prospect of a new heaven and a new earth. He isn't perfect, but he moves upright through the world as a citizen of God's kingdom because he accepts his sufferings on this earth as opportunities to grow in holiness and love. He does not adopt a stance that waits for purgatory to allow God to burn off his imperfections (a stance I'm quite fond of); instead he has abandoned himself to God's cleansing fire even now, and this is evidenced in how he treats his children, his family and friends, his colleagues, and especially his enemies. More than anything, I am mystified by his ability to forgive and to completely withhold judgment from even the greatest, most obvious offenders. He forgives, though they know not what they do. He has managed to bear the stigmata in a hidden way. The humility and love that this requires is so rare and so precious that in its presence, one can only reel with conviction and beg for mercy from above.

There *are* people who move through our world with an upright grace; there *is* holiness and righteousness and humility walking among us, and when we find it, we are encountering men and women and children who are living their purgatory on earth. They live with a saint's awareness that *the harvest is coming, prepare, make heavenly use of your suffering.* And this world continues to turn because of them.

Hell: The Face of a Rejected God

Have you ever noticed how much easier it is to catch a glimpse of hell on earth than a glimpse of heaven? When I first moved back to the Midwest, long overdue for a haircut, I found a local salon and booked the first appointment they had. The woman who cut my hair was stylish and very bright, and I couldn't help wondering about her: there was some deep seriousness hard won in her, something lurking beneath her bubbly, coifing veneer. As she chirped on about giving my hair "volume and movement," I started to ask her a few questions about herself. Before long, the whole story came spilling out. She'd left a burgeoning career as a family therapist after she'd taken just one too many cases involving child abuse.

Her final case involved a woman who routinely sold her daughter on the street, rented her out by the hour. That evil business venture came to an abrupt end one night when the child was murdered.

Hell is prideful and vain; it is ravenous to be seen. Every once in a while, it cannot contain itself for desiring attention and has to explode violently and flagrantly, a vomiting volcano, like a spoiled child who's had too much candy, just to be sure we don't miss it. And its own blatant flaunting and lack of dignity makes it even more ashamed and angry, so it explodes again and again in futile attempts to douse its own gnashing pain.

Paul said, "Set your minds on things that are above, not on things that are on earth." Hell doesn't like that line very much; hell doesn't like to have its thunder stolen. It will compete with heaven—to the death—to win your attention, if not your affection.

When we think of eternal hell, we can easily picture its murdering inhabitants. If someone asks us who goes to hell, post-office mug shots flash before our eyes. We picture Hitler and child killers and Idi Amin. But I don't think that's the right question to be asking. Maybe the more useful question to ask ourselves is: *Will I go to hell?*

Here is my answer: I hope not.

Oh, but sometimes, I have to wonder at the hardness of my own, stony, willful, unforgiving heart. My heart that too often just wants her own way, to be left alone.

It's easy to imagine our friends and loved ones enjoying eternity with us, greeting us at the pearly gates in all joy and celebration. But what if we get there and just as we are about to cross the threshold, our worst enemy appears, the one who hurt us the most, betrayed us or used us, abandoned us in our greatest hour of need, the one who wrought so much pain, we didn't think we'd survive it. Maybe we didn't.

There they are, all smiles and beautiful and joyful and welcoming *you*, like they have any business at all being in heaven. This one you said you'd never forgive, the one that makes you stop, right there, at the entrance to paradise and say, "*Oh no*, not if *she's* in there! No way, not if *he* made it in." And to the saints and angels gathered about, we launch our final protest: "Don't you know what they did to me?"

Then what? Imagine that you were the murdered child and your mother who betrayed you in the worst possible way, unto death, is the first to greet you in heaven. Would you still want heaven if even *she* got in? If given the choice, heaven with your enemy whom you *must* forgive, or hell left only to yourself and your own brooding, what would you choose?

Of all the criminals that might keep us from entering eternal blessedness, I think resentment must be the number one offender, along with his partner in crime, self-justification. "If you only knew how hard it is to be me." We can acknowledge our greed, lust, gluttony, dishonesty, faithlessness, and many other sins. But when it comes to "forgive them, they know *not* what they do," oh, dear, Lord, *have mercy on me*. It is more than I can manage on my own.

It might be tenable for someone who demonstrated some contrition, or at the very least admitted their crime, but the prayer which fell from the lips of Jesus was not, *Forgive them because they are really, really sorry*. No. They don't know the extent of the damage they've caused, and maybe, this side of eternity, they never will. If it comes to this, giving this up, acknowledgment of how deeply we have been wounded, would we do it?

Let's thoughtfully consider one more aspect to the prayer of Jesus. When does he pray it? After two years of therapy, or a trip to Bermuda to relax and recover? No, at the moment of greatest torment and pain, in the very midst of the betrayal. "Forgive them, Father, they have no idea the damage they are causing *in this very moment.*" We have noted that love is the greatest evidence that heaven is real. "Forgive them, they know not what they do" is also compelling evidence that hell is real, too, because it lays out the price to be paid for escaping it in absolutely naked, cold blood. "Forgive them, they know not what they do" lives fearlessly with perfect eternal perspective.

I once had a spiritual director who told me that every relationship I have is really about the relationship I have with God. When I was tempted to imagine myself judge and jury of those closest to me or, on the other hand, fear what someone else thought about me, he would remind me that I didn't know what God was up to in other people. And even if I did, it wasn't my business; that was between the other person and God. There was enough to worry about keeping my own side of the street clean. Our final judgment is *our* final judgment and no one else's. There will be no one else standing there when the accounting of my life is taken, just me before my almighty maker and friend. We've been given the capacity to see sin and name it. And the first place that we do that—not only recognizing and naming sin but also uprooting and annihilating it with radical help from heaven—is in ourselves.

Blessed Mother Teresa once said that if you knew everyone's story, you'd love everybody. Ultimately, I need to trust that the justice of God is perfect. Only God knows the whole story, everyone's whole story, including mine, by heart. If I meet someone in heaven who once upon a time ago hurt me, whatever pain remains between us will have already been healed to perfection, and we will see each other as heaven sees us. The joy in seeing one another's final rendering, especially those of our enemies, must be magnificent and overwhelming.

There is this to keep in mind, too: should I get to heaven and the one who hurt me the most shows up to welcome me in, I can only imagine how humbled and honored and awed I might feel to do the same—welcome into paradise the one I hurt the most.

HOLY FEAR AND TREMBLING

Just as heaven is a real place about which Jesus taught, so too is hell, and you don't want to make your eternal home in the latter. Regis Martin writes that "nothing exists in this world to equal the horror"[17] of eternal separation from God. The loneliness, suffering, and rage that rips through such a place must be more searing than a thousand suns, and that's why Jesus warns us so sternly about it.

Jesus was very clear about how we need to eradicate daily fear from our daily lives, but there was one fear that he actually promoted. We remember his instruction: "Do not fear those who kill the body but cannot kill the soul; rather fear him who can destroy both soul and body in hell" (Matthew 10:28). Hell means our soul destruction. It is, as Regis Martin writes, "to burn [your] last bridge with God," and "a final sundering of man from God, the utmost catastrophe ever to threaten man."[18] And the Lamb would do anything to prevent it. How incomprehensible is it, then, that God should create humankind with "a liberty so radical that it can choose its own annihilation"?[19] He would do anything but remove our free will to keep us from the gates of hell.

So, there's a choice to be made. It rests with you and you alone. And here's some more news: either destination you choose, it's going to hurt. Though the nature of the pain will be vastly different.

A friend was telling me about a book he'd read on healing after marital infidelity. Of all betrayals, I think that would be one of the most difficult to forgive, and in the book, there was a chapter devoted to addressing this particular issue. Its title was "But I Can't Forgive Him." When you opened to the first page of that chapter, you found only one single line: "You mean you *won't* forgive him." How plain and practical, how simple, just like the last things. Forgiveness is a choice we make, an action we take, sometimes again and again and again, until it sticks.

While working on an article about Our Lady of Kibeho, I had the chance to interview Immaculée Iligabiza, author of *Left to Tell*, which chronicles her experience surviving the Rwandan genocide. In 1994, Hutu rebels killed an estimated 77 percent of the Tutsi population of Rwanda, approximately eight hundred thousand people, including everyone in Iligabiza's family except for one brother. The horrors she survived are unimaginable, but one of the most compelling moments came when Immaculée visited the man who killed one of her brothers—literally chopping him to death with a machete—to forgive him. "Forgiveness is all I have to offer," she writes.[20] Clear and simple, in that impossible moment,

Iligabiza chose heaven. And freedom. She would not be a slave to resentment and revenge; she would be a citizen of heaven.

We want so much to place the responsibility elsewhere. We want to make God or our parents or lovers or friends or enemies responsible for how we end up, for who we become. And at different points of our life, they do share some responsibility. Still, ultimately, there's a choice to be made: purification and heaven, or hell. The pains of our purification—like learning to truly forgive—are passing and merciful, even if very, very great. Souls in purgatory know that heaven, eventually, awaits their arrival. But the pains of hell do not pass away. They churn and churn and grasp and devour. There is no escape from this dreadful, lonely, endless isolation.

Hell so often conjures up images of a vengeful, hateful God, but this is really a tragically misinformed image. "Whoever goes to hell," writes Martin, "takes himself there." Those who choose hell are the ones writhing with hatred, refusing to love, and wriggling to loose themselves from God's loving grip. Consider this passage from novelist George Bernanos:

No one is cast into Hell unless he has first thrust aside and drawn away from the terrible but gentle hand of God without having felt its grip. No one is abandoned unless he has committed the essential sacrilege of denying not the justice but the love of God. For the terrible Cross of wood may stand at the first dividing of the ways in our life to admonish us gravely and severely, but the last image we see before we take ourselves away forever is that other Cross of flesh, the two outstretched arms of the grievously suffering Friend, when the highest angel turns away in terror from the Face of a rejected God.[21]

When St. John of the Cross writes, "At the evening of life, we shall be judged on our love," this is what he means: Justice is not our real problem; no, the real problem is, and has always been, love.

The eternal invitation to the holy harvest ball has been issued. It will not, nor cannot, be rescinded; only rejected. Handwritten in the perfect, ancient script of holy Zion, it reads: *Beloved* [insert your name here], *will you love me and let me love you, forever, unto eternity?*

That is the question, the *last* question.

1. Adrienne von Speyr, *Mystery of Death* (San Francisco: Ignatius Press, 1988), 120–121.

2. Regis Martin, *The Last Things: Death, Judgment, Heaven, Hell* (San Francisco: Ignatius Press, 1998), 18.

3. Hans Urs von Balthasar, *A Short Primer for Unsettled Laymen* (San Francisco: Ignatius Press, 2004), 2.

4. Balthasar, *The Glory of the Lord, Volume 1, Seeing the Form,* trans. Erasmo Leiva-Merikakis (San Francisco: Ignatius Press, 1982), 2.

5. Quoted by Regis Martin in "The Anguish of an Absence," reproduced by *30 Days, No.* 3 (1994): 45.

6. G. K. Chesterton, *Orthodoxy* (New York: Image Books, Doubleday, 2001), 8–9.

7. Flannery O'Connor, *Spiritual Writings* (Maryknoll, NY: Orbis Books, 2003), 66–67.

8. Denise Levertov, "On a Theme from Julian's Chapter XX,"

Selected Poems, ed. Paul A. Lacey (New York: New Directions Books, 2002), 152–153.

9. Augustine, *City of God against the Pagans*, ed. and trans. R. W. Dyson (New York: Cambridge University Press: 1998), 19:24.

10. Pope Benedict XVI, *Spe salvi*, Vatican City: Libreria Editrice Vaticana, (30 November 2007): 33.

11. Martin, 77.

12. Martin, 81.

13. Pope Benedict XVI, 34.

14. Scott Hahn, *Lamb's Supper: The Holy Mass as Heaven on Earth* (New York: Doubleday, 1999), 104.

15. Hahn, 105.

16. John Henry Newman, *Parochial and Plain Sermons* (San Francisco: Ignatius Press, 1987), 6, 8.

17. Martin, 127.

18. Martin, 116.

19. Martin, 114.

20. Immaculée Iligabiza, *Left to Tell: Discovering God Amidst the Rwandan Holocaust* (London: Hay House Inc., 2006), 204.

21. Georges Bernanos, *The Impostor*, trans. J. C. Whitehouse (Lincoln, NE: University of Nebraska Press, 1999), 82.

8.

Rest and Remembrance in

the City of God

Be still, and know that I am God!
—Psalm 46:10

So God blessed the seventh day and hallowed it, because on it God rested from all the work that he had done in creation.
—Genesis 2:3

The mystery
That there is anything, anything at all,
Let alone cosmos, joy, memory, everything,
Rather than void: and that, O Lord,
Creator, Hallowed One, You still,
Hour by hour sustain it.
—Denise Levertov, "Primary Wonder"

Just out of graduate school, I worked for a company that put the writings of the early Church fathers on a searchable CD-ROM. It was my job to comb through the thirty-seven volumes of Polycarp, Irenaeus, Augustine, and the like, looking for any words that had been scanned improperly and to create embedded links in each chapter so that the work could be searched. A monotonous and somewhat Herculean task, it groomed me well in the thinking of the early Church fathers, particularly surrounding the development of the Mass, the doctrine of the real presence, and other distinctively Catholic beliefs.

This project did much to bring me back to the Catholic Church, and for that I'm grateful. What it did not do was whet my appetite for the study of patristics. My early years of education were sorely lacking in classical training (no doubt spending countless hours watching *Gilligan's Island* was not a huge help either), and I found wading through the work difficult. Though I was drawn to and deeply stirred by the overarching truths the Fathers expressed, I felt profoundly removed from these ancient figures. Gathering up their thoughts across thirty-seven volumes was more tedious than joyful.

Years later when I returned to school for a master's in Catholic studies, on the roster of courses in my first semester was an entire class devoted to one, single, patristic work: St. Augustine's *The City of God against the Pagans*. In the R. W. Dyson translation, it is 1,182 pages (not including the introduction). It was written over the course of more than a decade, from 413 to 426. This was not a period of history in which I was particularly interested, but I felt drawn to the assignment of reading with such focus one singular work by such a singular individual. It would be, at the least, a promising intellectual exercise to reintroduce my brain to graduate level work and, at best, a fruitful spiritual discipline.

Augustine is a doctor of the Church and a saint; he was a prolific and passionate writer, and I trusted that he would accompany me through this exercise right from heaven. I went to the perpetual adoration chapel at my Church and addressed God and

Augustine on my knees, asking for greater clarity of thought and increased discipline for study while reminding them that I was a terrifically slow reader and would need a lot of extra help. Thus began my semester studying *City of God* with its famous author, St. Augustine of Hippo.

On the first day of class, the professor likened studying *City of God* to climbing a mountain, and the analogy was a good one. It was a relentless effort *up*. To cover the entire work in one semester meant reading about a hundred pages a week, which wasn't all that much if you were up on your paganism, Cicero, and Varro. (Remember, my idea of studying a classic was watching the professor make a transistor radio out of coconuts; there was no one named Varro or Cicero on *Gilligan's Island*.)

Week after week, I was struck by the enormity of the work, the incredible effort it must have required without the aid of computers or editors or searchable CDs. That Augustine could additionally manage to maintain his line of thinking and argumentation as well as he did over more than a decade was simply remarkable. His clarity of thought and powers of concentration must have been startling. In addition to this work, he was writing tirelessly on other topics and performing his duties as a bishop. *City of God* is a feat indeed.

Fortunately, the effort of mountain climbing is frequently rewarded with the glories of mountain summits, and this is true with Augustine's *magnum opus* as well. *City of God* begins as an exhaustive refutation, but it ends as an exhortation, that deep sigh of relief that climbers enjoy on reaching the pinnacle. And, of course, Augustine's pinnacle is paradise.

Augustine was challenged to write the work in response to those who suggested that if Christianity was what it promised, Rome would never have been sacked—and by Christians, to boot—in 410. The first ten books address this charge, often in unrelenting and repetitive fashion, concentrating on the utter failures of the "city of man" and paganism. The second half of the book shifts into a more pastoral tone and contains the renowned Book XIX, oft-quoted by political historians for Augustine's reflections on a well-ordered society. For all of the commentary on *City of God* as a master work in political history, which it is, it is also a stirring exhortation to order one's life toward heaven.

In the final chapters, in a mix of conjecture, imagination, and exegesis, Augustine explores heaven, its inhabitants, and what it means to inherit "eternal blessedness." A professor my younger brother once knew said that reading Augustine in English, as compared with the original Latin, was like playing Mozart on the kazoo. Even consigned to English as I am, the last two chapters are particularly lovely. He offers a succinct and moving description of heaven, writing, "There we shall rest and see, see and love, love and praise."

His finale, this heavenly arpeggio of resting, seeing, loving, and praising, hangs on a very important opening note, and for the incredibly hard working Augustine, we can trust that he did not use the word lightly. If this book you have in your hands has struck any chord about heaven in you and you in heaven, this is a good note to end on: one of the most important ways that we practice heaven, that we bring heaven to earth, is to *rest*, for all the other notes in the great eternal chord build upon it.

SEVENTH DAY REMEMBRANCE

Before you start envisioning yourself ensconced on the sofa with the remote control, be assured that's not the kind of rest that I'm talking about. Nor is it sleeping in on Sundays or taking more vacation time, though sleep and recreation are important. The rest of heaven is so much more than the absence of work, or a reduction in physical or mental activities, or zoning out in front of the television. The kind of rest I'm encouraging, the kind of rest that Augustine is referring to, is spiritual rest, sabbath rest, rest in God. Heaven's rest is Seventh Day rest.

And it has been built into the Master's plan from the beginning of time.

We've lost sight of this notion; keeping the Lord's Day holy has become passé, meant for a weaker people, a time with fewer technological advances and less sophistication. We'd rather have the conveniences of gyms and grocery stores and online trading available to us twenty-four hours a day, seven days a week. But we are simply not designed for such unrelenting activity. We have said that when we miss the Mass, we miss all of the grace of heaven. When we dismiss sabbath rest, we dismiss the promises of heaven as unnecessary.

The Church reminds us that the Sabbath is "a memorial of Israel's liberation from bondage in Egypt,"[1] and a "sign of the irrevocable covenant"[2] between God and man. The Sabbath is a celebration of the ways that God has remembered us and taken care of us, rescued us time and time again, ultimately through the cross. Think of that. He has remembered us—he remembers you—*irrevocably*. The awe that this truth should evoke in us when we are well-disposed to receive it—awe which rises up as an interior stillness and joy, awe that is given as a natural gift from God and nothing we've conjured on our own—is immeasurable. From the beginning, God ordered the whole of his creation, including his children, toward this sabbath rest of heaven: the rest of remembering *Holy, Holy, Holy Lord, God of power and might*. Augustine describes it this way:

> Then shall these words be fulfilled: "Be still, and know that I am God"; then shall be that great Sabbath which has no evening, which God celebrated among His first works, as it is written: "And God rested on the seventh day from all His works which He had made. And God blessed the seventh day, and sanctified it; because that in it He had rested from all His work."[3]

It bears repeating: God "celebrated [rest] among his first works." The summit of his creation was that deep sigh of rest; it was a designated, sanctified time to reflect on all that had been created. All of the unspeakable, unnameable, unimaginable energy and love required to create the entire universe, all that exists, culminates in rest and reflection and stillness before the Almighty One. Eternal rest is the active remembrance or recollection of God. How is it that we ever imagined we could, or should, reject regular participation in sabbath rest as optional?

In fact, sabbath rest was so important to the Lord that he made it a commandment. Keeping the Lord's Day holy is not the fourth *suggestion*, as we might like to imagine, it is the fourth *commandment*. There is holiness in sabbath rest; and it is critical that we understand what this means. When we thumb our noses at heaven's rest, it's like coming home after a hard day's work to find that our beloved has prepared an exquisite feast for us, and rather than sit down to enjoy and delight in the surprise, we toss it out into the street to rot and then go make ourselves a frozen TV dinner. Not only would such an action lay waste to all that is meant to nourish and sustain and delight us, it would break the heart of the preparer. It simply makes no sense at all not to keep the Lord's Day holy, (in the same way that it makes no psychological or spiritual sense not to keep *all* of the commandments).

In his day of rest, the Lord says, "Come and eat, *I* am the feast. Feast on *me*!" He says, "Feast on me in the Eucharist; feast on me in Scripture and sacred reading; feast on me in prayer and meditation; feast on me by contemplating the beauty of all that is created, including your loved ones. Feast on me in my justice, my mercy, and my love for you. Feast on *me*." This is the meaning of sabbath rest, resting in God. Do we accept this invitation issued from heaven, or do we casually toss him in the street and then go surf the Internet?

To reject this invitation is more than a rejection of God and the gift of heaven's rest; it is also a rejection of self. Rest is worked into the very nature of things, including the nature of God, as "creation was fashioned with a view to the sabbath."[4] If celebrating and keeping the sabbath is intrinsic to God's nature, it is also intrinsic to our own, since we are his creation, made in his image. Augustine speaks of heaven's rest this way (italics mine):

We ourselves shall become that seventh day, when we have been filled up and made new by His blessing and sanctification. *Then* shall we be still, and know that He is God: that *He is what we ourselves desired to be when we fell away from Him* and listened to the words of the tempter, "Ye shall be as gods," and so forsook God, Who would have made us as gods, not by forsaking Him, but *participating in Him . . . when we are restored by Him and perfected by His greater grace, we shall be still for all eternity, and know that He is God, being filled by Him when he shall be all in all.*

For it is only when we have understood that *all our good works are His*, and not our own, that *those works are credited to us for the attainment of that Sabbath rest. . . .* It is said by the prophet Ezekiel, "and I gave them my Sabbaths to be a sign between me and them, that they might know that I am the Lord that sanctifies them." We shall know this perfectly when we shall be perfectly at rest, and shall know perfectly that He is God.[5]

In heaven, we *become* Seventh Day Sabbath; we *become* praise and living worship; and we get there by recognizing through our honor of the Lord's Day that he is our all in all, the sole-purpose and soul-end of our resting, seeing, loving, and praising. We get there by recognizing that all our good works are his, not ours, and it is through these that we are given eternal rest. We come to sabbath rest to *remember*, to remember who God is and that he remembers us.

A Simple Heaven

Ironically, entering into rest can be a real battle. Our world is easily cluttered, and clutter, by its nature, is very unrestful. We need to keep teaching ourselves that empty space is a good thing, that maybe it isn't as empty as we think, that "the invisible has the strongest presence of all."[6]

Any kind of shopping quickly induces this state of unrest in me. I feel overwhelmed with too many options, and an unnecessary, unnatural, incessant, and almost evil pressure to constantly acquire things I simply do not need.

My aversion for shopping first became clear to me in 1990, when I was just out of college and made a pilgrimage to Medjugorje. At that time, pilgrims still frequently stayed in the homes of local townspeople, as I did, and there were very few vendors peddling their wares of rosaries and medals and holy cards. From the moment I arrived, I was struck by the simplicity in lifestyle for many in the area, and it was the clothing and shoe store that drove the point home.

Looking in the shop window, I remember noticing the shoes that were on display. There were two styles available, both black leather. In that moment, a distinct feeling of peacefulness, a restfulness washed over me: A or B. That was it. It was marvelously simple. And everyone had the same options.

It was precisely this simplicity that allowed me to relax into the experience of pilgrimage more deeply. Some of the crazy distractions and unreasonable expectations for what I should have and be and look like had been removed, and I wanted to hang on to that simplicity, that empty space where invisible holiness could creep in and set up house.

The *rest* of heaven is a little like this; not distracted, but gently and reasonably focused. Again, the rest of heaven is a remembering. The rest of heaven distills things in simplicity, and what rises to the surface of that reduction is that when we practice the rest of heaven, we remember God and his mighty works. We rest in the knowledge that God remembers his people.

LIFE IN CHAOS, SOUL AT REST

Of course, achieving this simplicity isn't always so simple. It is easy to practice sabbath rest when all is going well. And it's important that we do store up our consolations. But practicing simplicity and sabbath rest is no guarantee that your life will become a perpetual sunny-day picnic minus the ants. That's *ease*. That's not the kind of rest we aim for (though sometimes we do get sunny-day picnics minus the ants). We aim for soul-rest.

In recent years, I have made a far more pointed commitment to live in the service of the Church. However, as I discern how God might use me more and more, how I might point myself more concretely in the direction of heaven, my life has virtually unraveled. An engagement was broken, a book contract I'd hoped for did not materialize, and someone I trusted accused me of something I did not do. The pain of that betrayal was excruciating; the damage it has caused may never be repaired this side of paradise.

My quest for heaven was taking a radical beating, and practicing sabbath rest seemed almost ridiculous at times.

But brewing oh so subtly in the background, I heard angels at play and holy laughter. Somewhere, way down deep, beyond words, beyond sounds and senses, beyond my own overt despair and fear, there was joy and a soul at rest. Career and finances, books contracts and even broken hearts shall pass away. We know, don't we, that all things shall be made beautiful in their time. The looming question amidst all of it was this: did I, daily, in big and small ways, choose heaven?

Sadly, not often enough. Just ask my mother; more than most, she loved me at my absolute worst. One particular difficulty was how long my house languished unsold during one of the worst real estate downturns in recent history. Month after month went by as I tried to manage a property from fifteen hundred miles away. I had water in the basement, and then mold, a squirrel in the crawl space, and a vagrant apparently broke in and took a very dirty bath. After a year and a half on the market, an offer came in that was so low it was almost laughable, but it was all I had, and I was long since out of cash. As my attorney entered into nerve-wracking negotiations for a short sale, I was a basket case. Eventually, it looked like the deal would go through and the whole burden would finally be removed from my drooping, exhausted, and dead-broke shoulders.

Walking through my parents' kitchen one morning, my mom noted, "Well, it seems you are really on the upswing, and you very nearly handled it well." We both burst out laughing. Practicing that sabbath rest of heaven—that rest that remembers the mighty rescue of the Mighty One—feels like a Herculean task at times. I fail and fail and fail again. But that doesn't change the fact that heaven is right here. "Be still and know that I am God"—we may not get the "be still" portion, but it doesn't ever change that last part: "I am God." Yes, he is.

The house didn't sell, and my situation declined further still. One of my best girlfriends said, "It's making a woman out of you." Amen. Let's hope. Let's hope it's making a heavenly woman out of me.

I had a spiritual mentor who used to say, "Liz, sometimes life is scary because sometimes life is scary." I would add the corollary that sometimes life is complicated because sometimes life is complicated. The question remains simple: am I going to choose heaven or hell today? These are the options. There is no in-between. If you believe your Creed, if you mean those words you profess, "I believe in God, the Father Almighty, Creator of heaven and earth," that is the question for you. And taking sabbath rest seriously will always help you answer the question. It will slow you down long enough to *remember* the last part: "I am God."

Yes, Father, you are.

ONE SUNDAY IN SIENA

The bus would come at 7:00 a.m., so we were up early with bad coffee and bits of fruit and bread and packing lunches: a group of students, pilgrims for the day, on our way to spend a fall Sunday in beautiful Siena.

During the drive north from Rome to Tuscany, our chaplain read passages from St. Catherine's life and *Dialogues*. We prayed the office and, when we passed by, pondered the Eucharistic miracle of Orvieto, where a host bled and an unbelieving heart was pierced. We gazed out the window, taking in the rising hills and distant horizons, those views that are denied to your eyes living in the city. We prayed for sunshine and safe arrival, the simple things of daily life.

When we reached Siena, our first stop was San Domenico, the church where St. Catherine would often go to pray. We knelt in the chapel where she received many mystical visions. We hovered over the spot, memorialized in red stone, where she says the Lord gave her a new heart. We bowed and said our private prayers before some of her relics housed in the church and tried to take in the enormity of such a thing: the relic of a saint.

Then our chaplain gathered us up again, and we trailed after him as he took us deeper into Siena, making our way through the steep streets that drop and rise at crazy, erratic, breathtaking angles. The ancient city, having managed for ages to cling to the sharply sloped earth beneath it, somehow remained upright and beautiful.

Eventually we found our way to the Basilica di San Francesco, the church that houses and protects another Eucharistic miracle. As we gathered before its designated chapel on our knees, a sturdy, little Italian priest with a penchant for robustly rolling his *r*'s emerged to tell us the story while our chaplain translated.

In 1730, on the vigil of the feast of the Assumption, nearly four hundred hosts were stolen from the tabernacle, along with the gold ciborium that held them. When the theft was discovered the next morning at Mass, all of Siena mourned the sacrilege and many prayers were issued on behalf of their safe return. Several days later, the hosts were discovered in a donation box at another church. The ciborium, of course, was long gone.

The hosts were cleaned and returned in solemn procession to the basilica, where they have remained perfectly preserved for nearly three hundred years.[7] In the past century, when scrutinized by scientists, the hosts were found to be fresh bread, all remaining incorrupt. Several popes have made pilgrimages to the basilica, and Pope John Paul II declared that through these hosts Jesus was saying once again, "Courage, I am with you."

A little later in the day, we celebrated Mass before St. Catherine's crucifix—the one she was praying in front of when she received the stigmata. Kneeling there during the consecration, while the priest raised the host and the chalice, and heaven split open upon us, I thought that every inch of Italy was a living Sabbath, deep with remembering. But this moment—"Do this in memory of me"—this moment covers the earth, the whole earth, in the sabbath rest of heaven.

"This mystery," writes Fr. Benedict Groeschel, "lights up the whole earth and sky. It sanctifies places far away from where it is reserved."[8] And this is why Augustine insists that we rest and see, see and love, love and praise. This is why our sabbath rest centers on the Paschal Feast. The apostles begged their friend, their Messiah, "Stay with us." And he did. He does. He never abandons his own. He stays with us, so our hearts can rest in him.

FALLING DOWN IN ADORATION

Before we left the basilica of the Eucharistic miracle, we were
granted a rare privilege I shall never forget. "Here, one adores,"
said the Italian priest. "Here, one prays. Blessed are your eyes
for being able to see what others cannot see." And with that he
turned and headed off toward the tabernacle. While we sang *Tantum ergo* and "Jesus, remember me," each one of us was able to
stand in solitude for a moment before this extraordinary miracle
exposed. Aquinas said that contemplation is the "simple act of
gazing at the truth," and there we were, face to face in a mutual
exchange, not Jesus on display like some dead thing mounted
on a pedestal. This was a living exchange with the Living Water,
meeting, in utter simplicity, in startling intimacy, the whole gaze
of heaven. I could barely raise my eyes, because there he was,
Truth looking back.

After we had all had our private moment of adoration, the
faithful little priest, so fervent a guardian of this miracle, knelt
with us and recited what I imagine were some of the only lines
of Scripture that he knew in English, but they were more than
enough. In a thick Italian accent, he said, "And the Word was
made flesh and dwelt among us," and "I am the Bread from
heaven."

Before he gave us the final blessing with the monstrance, he
tried his English again, and we repeated his phrases like little children: "Good-bye, Jesus, be with us . . . and we be with you!"

Then he held up two fingers and said, "I leave you two things."
Though he was addressing the whole group, it seemed like he was

looking straight at me when he said with great, reverent deliberation, "Remember this miracle you have seen today. And be missionaries; share what you have learned here." When we bowed our heads and he blessed us in the name of the Father, the Son, and the Holy Spirit, I knew it was not the priest who was asking, it was the triune God before us. Jesus was asking, the Father was asking, and the Holy Spirit was asking. *Remember what you have seen here today*, they said. *Remember me.*

Yes, Father, I replied. *I will.*

We will. Your Church remembers you, Bread of Heaven.

1. *Catechism of the Catholic Church* (Vatican City: Libreria Editrice Vaticana, 1997), 2170.

2. *Catechism*, 2171.

3. Augustine, *City of God against the Pagans*, ed. and trans. R. W. Dyson (New York: Cambridge University Press, 1998), 22:30.

4. *Catechism*, 347.

5. Augustine, 22:30.

6. Daniel O'Leary, "Space for Grace," *The Tablet* (November 18, 2006), 15.

7. Normally, in such a circumstance, the hosts would have been immediately consumed upon their discovery. Some suggest that because the Siennese wanted to come and pay their respects before the holy hosts due to the sacrilege they suffered, the priests did not consume them right away. Whatever the reason, the Franciscans in charge who allowed them to remain uneaten began to notice that the hosts simply did not deteriorate.

8. Benedict Groeschel and James Monti, *In the Presence of Our Lord: The History, Theology, and Psychology of Eucharistic Devotion* (Huntington, IN: Our Sunday Visitor, 1997), 289.

9.

Closing Exhortation:

All the Way to Heaven

"Teacher, what must I do to inherit eternal life?"

Two times they come to him, looking for eternity's formula. Two times this question is posed to the strange and mysterious carpenter, this Nazarene; once by a rich young man with many possessions, and again by a lawyer who wants to prove himself righteous before the crowds. Two times they ask him, the Messiah: "Teacher, what must I do to inherit eternal life?" (see Matthew 19:16-30; Luke 18:18-30; and Luke 10:25-37).

On both counts, it was a bold move.

I, for one, am so glad they asked. Jesus teaches us so many important things about heaven in his replies.

In both cases, he first points us to the basics, as though he were teaching young children their letters. He clearly outlines the daily call of a life of discipleship: keep the commandments; love God with your whole heart, mind, and soul; love your neighbor as yourself. To the lawyer he adds that most memorable and beautiful story of the Good Samaritan, and we are reminded to take action in the face of injustice, to be merciful, to go above and beyond in our care for the lowly, vulnerable, and downtrodden.

To the rich young man, however, his additional instructions were a little different. Jesus tells this man to sell all his possessions, distribute the proceeds among the poor, and then he issues a most intriguing invitation: "Come, follow me."

We all know the rich young man's response. Who among us cannot relate to it in some way, feeling the grief in his sunken shoulders? Who among us does not possess something that, even for the kingdom, we are reluctant to surrender? His instructions may be simple, but they are demanding. His invitation lays claim to our whole life, our whole heart, our whole soul.

But don't we also adore heaven all the more for asking so much of us?

Think of it this way: A child whose parents have no expectations of him knows it, even if only subconsciously, and this knowledge crushes his spirit. A child whose parents have no expectations of her will deliver exactly that in life: nothing. But then there's the parent who does have hope in the child, who believes in her capacity for true heroism because—didn't the passage also say "all things are possible with God"? That parent turns to her and says, "Give it your all; give all you have to give; love with all your heart; do more, not less; look to a task and ask 'what is the most of myself that I might give?' not 'what's the least I can do to get by?'" *That* child will groan, and bloom. That child is being nurtured in hope and ordered toward heaven. That child is covered by a love beyond the walls of this world.

That's the kind of parent we have in our heavenly Father. That's the kind of love Jesus came to profess. If Jesus had turned to the rich young man and said, "No worries, friend, you're doing just fine," we would have recoiled at the pandering, the lowering of the bar. Jesus always knew perfectly who among the crowd needed mercy and who needed chastisement, who needed forgiveness and who needed a firm hand. Either way, he always gave gifts of love, never watered-down approval. To do the latter would have been to practice the bland kind of cowardice we call "indifference." As if to say, "it really doesn't matter that much." What you do, how you live, what you believe, what you love, how you love, who you are—nothing matters more. You matter, and this is why Jesus gave his life. His hopes for us are big hopes, eternal hopes—and this is an unspeakable grace. It gives us our dignity.

While I have little hope for the poor lawyer who wanted to appear righteous, I have a suspicion that that rich young man went home and thought things over. My little wish is that he went home and prayed and pondered. As the words of Jesus that day clung to him, wrapping snugly around his heart, they began to heat up and melt the tight grasp he had on so many things.

Maybe his possessions were objects—camels and jewels and condos in all the right vacation spots. Maybe they were interior possessions—great intellectual feats or pride or self-assurance, self-reliance, imagining himself "a self-made man." Maybe he simply possessed other plans for his future than, "Come, follow me."

Come, follow me. Jesus knew what he was asking. He knows full well our capacities. When he turned to that rich young man with those words, he had more hope in the young man than the young man had in himself. There's a reason the poet writes, "Hope springs *eternal.*"

Come, follow me. Every day, it called a little more, bled a little more deeply into the young man's heart. Still, he knew that to accept it was something he could not do on his own. He wrestled within himself; he thought many times, "Why did I ever open my big mouth?" But I think his heart was sincere, his questions asked in earnest, and the challenging response of our Lord lingered with him in love and highest, holiest hope until its work was completed.

Come, follow me. One day, the rich young man woke up, beaming and jubilant and pierced and *decided.* He bolted from his bed chamber and burst into the courtyard of his well-appointed abode, and raising his fists as if in victory, he shouted to the other still sleeping inhabitants of his fine home, "Let's go to heaven!"

And before he could even begin to empty the contents of his cupboards or his hubris, there was much rejoicing in paradise.

Sometimes, I think we tend to take this passage from Scripture as solely referring to those called to religious life, and those are high callings, to be sure. But sometimes I think we only *wish* it were meant *only* for priests and monks and nuns and celibates and the Blessed Mother Teresa and her armies of missionaries. Christ's invitation, *Come, follow me,* must find its way into every Christian life, every Christian vocation, because this is how we study for eternity. *Come, follow me,* begins now—not later—for all of us. It is an eternal request; our answer, an eternal disposition, a decision to live with eternal perspective and to live lives of great, fearless love. It is the way to heaven. "All the way to Heaven is Heaven," we remember from St. Catherine, "because Christ is the way."

No work in all of Rome is more moving to me than Michelangelo's *Pietà.* Despite its location in such a bustling area of St. Peter's, I have spent long hours in contemplation of this piece.

Its grace-filled lines, its tenderness and truth, draw me back to it again and again until, I hope, the beauty of its form has been impressed upon me. I long to know it interiorly—not in my mind, but to know it by heart.

What the *Pietà* makes so plain is that love isn't a feeling; it is an action, a decision captured by Michelangelo in marble. Jesus (along with the Blessed Mother) made a decision to love. His feelings didn't send him tripping happily along *la via crucis*. No, "let this cup pass," sprang from that human heart, but this was not the final word. His entreaty was fully surrendered to "not my will but yours be done." *Jesus made a decision*, a decision to love, a decision for heaven. Every day we must do the same. Every day we must rise from our sleep, thank the Lord for another day's chance to grow in holiness, and plant ourselves firmly in the trajectory that leads "all the way to heaven."

"Those who have talked us out of our belief in heaven," writes Joseph Ratzinger, "or would like to talk us out of it, have not given us the earth in exchange but have made it desolate and empty, have covered it with darkness. We must find once more the courage to believe in eternal life with all our heart."[1]

It takes courage, boldness. It takes a decision to love.

Do not doubt that the invitation is as real as the book in your hands. In fact, it is much more so. You are wanted. You are deeply, eternally desired. Desired so greatly, so ardently by the Father that he sent his most beloved Son to take on flesh and sin, to reunite heaven and earth, to heal you and bring you home.

Jesus comes and calls. He calls you from heaven; he calls you to heaven. He knows the way by heart.

Still, you're a little frightened, a little on edge.

Courage, Jesus says, *I am with you.* He knows your fear.

Still, you wonder, could it be true? Could he possibly hope, *eternally hope*, for someone like me?

You want to be sure. You want to draw closer. So you step forward, you step out from the crowd, you lean in with your heart until, suddenly, he turns to meet you. And before you have asked your most earnest question, the truth in his eyes is burning right through you, burning away your fear, inviting you to step into eternity, into absolute love. Maybe you step back—it's all too much—but just then you notice Mary and the angels and saints all around him, that holy, beaming Church, their prayers and wisdom, warm and ancient beneath your unsteady feet. You breathe; you step forward once again, and look up to find that his eyes have not left you for a moment. And when you return the gaze of the Lamb, before one word is spoken, you find you have been pierced. He is piercing you, heart to heart, with joy.

Beloved, he says, *come, follow me. All the way to heaven.*

1. Joseph Ratzinger, *Co-Workers of the Truth: Meditations for Every Day of the Year*, ed. Irene Grassi (San Francisco: Ignatius Press, 1992), 356.